D0591039

# THINK LIKE A
# WINNER

Best wishes,
Yehuda Shinar

I dedicate this book to my mother and to my daughters, Yarden and Danielle, whom I love so much, and to their mother, Iris.

A special place in my heart is kept and dedicated to Admiral Samuel Tankus from whom one literally never stops learning something, usually about oneself. He taught me the importance of thinking like a winner in creating the power to control and shape your own destiny, no matter what.

# THINK LIKE A WINNER

Yehuda Shinar

**Vermilion**
LONDON

1 3 5 7 9 10 8 6 4 2

Published in 2007 by Vermilion, an imprint of Ebury Publishing

A Random House Group company

The Random House Group Limited Reg. No. 954009

Addresses for companies within the Random House Group can be found at
www.randomhouse.co.uk

A CIP catalogue record for this book is available from the British Library

The Random House Group Limited makes every effort to ensure that the papers used in its books are made from trees that have been legally sourced from well-managed and credibly certified forests. Our paper procurement policy can be found on
www.randomhouse.co.uk

Printed and bound in Great Britain by
Clays Ltd, St Ives plc

ISBN 9780091912901

Copies are available at special rates for bulk orders. Contact the sales development team on 020 7840 8487 for more information.

To buy books by your favourite authors and register for offers, visit
www.rbooks.co.uk

**Mixed Sources**
Product group from well-managed forests and other controlled sources
www.fsc.org  Cert no. TT-COC-2139
FSC  © 1996 Forest Stewardship Council

# CONTENTS

# ACKNOWLEDGEMENTS

To my dear family, who were tremendously supportive and considerate throughout the whole process of writing this book.

To Dan Rookwood, who helped me to turn my life's work into this book. He represents the winning model so beautifully: he never gives up even when it gets really tough; he's a wonderful and challenging thinker; and he's brilliantly skilled.

To Julia Kellaway, my editor at Vermilion, for her wisdom and clarity, her outstanding talent and professionalism and, above everything else, the great atmosphere she created during the writing process.

To Tony Faulkner, my good friend and Winning representative in the UK. There are not enough words to describe Tony's efficiency, his variety of skills and his extraordinary winning spirit.

# FOREWORD

When I became coach of the England rugby team, I had one goal: to win the World Cup as the top-ranked side. So I worked back from that ultimate aim. To that end, I was prepared to look at anything that I thought might give us an advantage over our competitors. That's how I came to meet Yehuda Shinar.

A business friend of mine told me about how Yehuda had developed a programme aimed at teaching people how to be winners that was getting some impressive results. I thought it was worth looking at so, with an open mind, I flew to Israel to stay with him for a few days.

I was amazed. Not because anything Yehuda was saying was particularly revelatory; if anything, quite the opposite. I was amazed at how simple it was. The most successful things in life are often the most simple – perhaps because they are less likely to go wrong. Yehuda had decoded the apparently complicated art of winning into a basic science. He was explaining everything I'd ever experienced and done when I was successful in a competitive environment, both in sport and in business. But up until then, I wasn't actually aware of precisely what I was doing when I was succeeding or, for that matter, when I was failing. By developing my awareness and self-understanding, I saw that I could increase my frequency of success and decrease my frequency of failure. I'd just never heard anyone stating so simply and clearly what were obvious truths about winning. It was exactly the link I'd been searching for.

Although Yehuda didn't know anything about rugby, I felt that we could use his model for our purposes. So I brought him across to work with my coaches. We needed to think about coaching in a new and different way. As a nation we have the potential to achieve outstanding results in so many areas, but we consistently fail to maximise that potential. I knew we needed to change our mentality, our mindset – even our culture – if we wanted to be the best in the world.

Yehuda had drawn up a list of what he called winning behaviours – areas like maintaining momentum, developing self-control, thinking correctly under pressure, continuously analysing and debriefing our performances. I'd never looked at most of these before as clear and obvious aspects that could be measured, controlled and coached. We had the winning behaviour principles condensed into seven posters, each focusing on a different part of the game. We even had the key points emblazoned across the walls and ceiling in the England dressing room at Twickenham. Together it formed a tight, coherent, focused strategy.

The results speak for themselves. We increased our frequency of winning dramatically to arrive at the World Cup as the favourites and top-ranked team. And when the players really needed to think clearly under pressure, they did it. I am not saying that Yehuda won us the World Cup – but he was an important part of the team for a period of time when I was developing our strategy to communicate what winning actually meant to players and coaches alike.

The beauty of Yehuda's model is its simplicity and adaptability. Whether you want to be more successful in sport, in business or in your personal life, I believe you can adapt Yehuda's model to make you think like a winner; to give you that crucial advantage over others.

I hope this book will give you the satisfaction of overcoming your weaknesses and achieving what you have always dreamed about but never thought possible.

We ended up achieving our ultimate aim – and Yehuda's model was part of that success. I am confident that what you will read in this book will allow you to draw up your own game plan, to actively maximise your potential and so meet your personal goals. I wish you every success.

Sir Clive Woodward, OBE
London, 2007

# PREFACE

## WHY I HAVE WRITTEN THIS BOOK

I am a winning coach. I run a company in Israel called Winning Enterprises dedicated to helping people like you maximise their potential, be successful and win.

My job is varied. Over the past 18 years I have worked with all sorts of people: housewives, fighter pilots, opera singers, small business owners, footballers and high-flying bank executives. I've been credited with being the man behind the success of many famous people. Just as rewardingly, I've also helped many more regular people achieve the kinds of success and happiness in their lives that they never dreamed possible.

I started my company almost by accident. Back in the early 1990s I was working as an analyst for the personnel departments of various business clients who wanted to find out the suitability of the applicants for their job vacancies. As we all know, organisations can fall or flourish depending on whom they employ. Choose the right person from the outset and huge mistakes can be averted and money can be saved. My office tested and analysed the candidates and evaluated their potential in order to help companies make the best appointments.

Each client seemed to want to know pretty much the same thing: will this candidate be a 'winner'? However, they all had very different ideas of what a winner was. There was no consensus as to the attributes that make up a winner. For example, some clients perceived winners to be those candidates who were strong-minded and decisive with obvious leadership potential. Others perceived them to be open-minded, creative and with a desire to learn. So I decided to see if I could decode what makes someone a winner, what makes them successful.

In 2006, I was given perhaps my most unusual challenge to date. I was asked by the Scottish Institute of Sport Foundation to be a part of their programme to try to neutralise the Scottish people's negative outlook on life that has become their national stereotype.

It soon struck me that this attitude wasn't unique to Scotland, or even to Britain – although it is probably true that having a fairly negative or cynical outlook on life is part of British culture. Negativity is something that affects people all around the world to varying degrees, though sometimes we might not even realise it. Compelled to take on the ambitious commission to help change Scotland's unhealthily pessimistic mindset, I decided to write a manual to go along with it that would apply to people anywhere in the world. This is that manual.

I have already enjoyed dramatic success in counteracting a defeatist mentality on a smaller scale. Most famously, I worked with coach Clive Woodward to turn the England rugby team from nearly-men into winners; winners of the 2003 World Cup, no less. It wasn't because I am some master tactician – I know very little about rugby – but because, through Clive and his coaches, I was able to instil winning behaviour patterns into the players. That relatively localised success had a huge feel-good effect in England. All of a sudden there was a groundswell of pride and a feeling of invincibility among English people again. Winning is a powerful experience.

The result of my years of research and analysis is a formula for identifying and producing winners. The beauty of this formula is its simplicity, adaptability and universal applicability. It is not something that takes years of hard work to perfect; nor is it something that only an elite few can use. I have always felt that my work is for everyone, and so writing this book is the best way of getting my message across to the widest possible audience.

This is a manual for success that I firmly believe has distilled the essence of winning and turned it into a skill that can be easily learned, practised and used to turn anyone into one of life's winners. And yes – that includes you.

Yehuda Shinar
Israel, 2007

# INTRODUCTION

## WHY YOU SHOULD READ THIS BOOK

Do you...

▶ wish you had more self-confidence?

▶ sometimes panic under pressure?

▶ often wish you had more time?

▶ wish you didn't put things off?

▶ ever doubt yourself and wish you were more assertive?

▶ ever have negative thoughts?

▶ feel afraid of failure?

▶ wish you had more control of your life?

▶ want to perform better in one-to-one situations?

▶ wish you were better in relationships?

▶ want to improve at giving presentations and explaining your thoughts?

▶ wish you could do things you think you're no good at?

▶ wish that you didn't worry and get so stressed?

▶ want people to respect you more?

▶ wish other people properly appreciated you?

▶ want to be liked by more people?

▶ wish you were more organised?

▶ ever feel frustrated or jealous that you are not as successful as other people you know?

▶ ever feel too daunted even to dare take on a big challenge that is really important to you?

1

Do you wish you could answer 'no' to more of these questions?

If you honestly answered 'no' to all of those questions, then congratulations. You don't need this book so give it to a friend before you make it all dog-eared.

If you answered 'yes' to some or indeed all of those questions, then this book is for you. In fact, it's a book that could very positively change your life.

# YOU ARE A WINNER

You might not feel like a winner yet. However, if you follow the advice and tips you're about to read, I guarantee that you will immediately start to become one. This is because you've got what it takes to be a winner in you right now; you just don't yet know how to unlock that part of you. I'm going to show you how to do just that. How? Put very basically, I'm going to teach you how to recognise what you do right when you succeed, and also what you do wrong when you fail. This is so that you can repeat what you did right over and over and thus dramatically reduce the frequency of failure. It really is that simple and anyone can do it.

The idea of being a winner might be an alien concept to you. You might not even find it all that attractive as it may smack of some kind of testosterone-fuelled competition. What I'm talking about here is success and happiness in life. In that respect we all want to be winners. We all want to be successful; to be happy; to be lucky. We all want our dreams to come true, and to feel like we have more control over our lives. These are not just wants; they are basic human needs – they are what drive us.

Let's put the cat among the pigeons straight away with some bold statements you perhaps won't agree with. But by the end of the book, I think you will.

▶ You don't need to be naturally talented to be a winner.

▶ You don't need to be hyper-intelligent to do well.

▶ You don't need to be highly skilled to be successful.

▶ You don't need to be rich to have an advantage in life.

Of course all these things can help, but whoever you are and whatever it is you want to achieve, you can quite easily be one of life's winners – irrespective of natural talent, intelligence and great skill. Many people believe success can be bought – the winning principles outlined in this book testify to the fact that it can't.

This is the controversial and thrilling promise and premise on which I have developed my model for achieving success. It's a model that has revolutionised the lives of all who have adopted it, men and women of all ages and backgrounds. And it will do the same for you, no matter who you are.

## SOMETHING BORROWED, SOMETHING NEW

Yes, these winning principles are new. But what they are actually based on is far from original. Purposely so; that is their strength. We're not reinventing the wheel here; we're just making it a faster, smoother, more enjoyable ride. The winning formula is founded on tried-and-tested methods of achieving success, and then replicating it.

Rather like a genetic engineer might isolate the gene that makes a carrot orange in order to develop and use it to make other things orange, so I have isolated the characteristics, thinking patterns and behaviours that make winners out of people. This has been the result of 18 years' research and refinement and thousands of case studies around the world. Furthermore, I have devised a method of transplanting that success in all spheres of life. So it can help you in your profession, your personal relationships, your ability to pay the gas bill on time – anything.

In my research of over 3,000 individuals from all cultures and backgrounds I compiled a database of common winning characteristics. After a while, I discovered significant trends – patterns of thinking. I developed and tested these trends in training all manner of people over a period of years. These were my guinea pigs. The results were always consistent. When their patterns of thinking were expertly developed, their personal performance increased in every circumstance. These people became winners.

## RAISING AWARENESS OF SUCCESS AND FAILURE

What does a winner actually do in practice in order to fulfil their potential so effectively and so often? Is there a secret to achieving such remarkable results, sometimes against the odds? There's no big secret here. The only surprise is that there is no surprise. The winning behaviours are more or less the very same strategies you make use of from time to time when you succeed – even if it's actually only by accident.

So if you already use these winning techniques, what's the big deal? Why are you reading a book about this if it's all common sense? And why have I written a whole book about it? The answer is: awareness.

The more I work with creating winners and helping winners win more often, the more I discover that the vast majority of people have no idea what they are doing when they succeed. But when they are made aware of the behaviours that help them succeed, they can enjoy success much more frequently. If you catch a fish by fluke, you won't know how to catch one again. If you learn why you caught the fish, you will know how to catch more, and your chances of doing so will increase hugely as a result.

It's all about eradicating chance. If you can deliberately choose the right, relevant winning behaviours because you are aware of what the right, relevant winning behaviours are, then you can reliably duplicate your successes. But if you're not aware of why you have succeeded in the past and instead rely on intuition, supposed luck or chance – or sticking with what you have always done before, irrespective of whether or not it is the right method – then you'll never increase the frequency of your successes.

The same holds true in regard to failure. If you are aware of the factors and reasons that explain why you lose, you can avoid making those same mistakes again, thus reducing your chances of failure. Simply by cutting out the 'behaviours' that make us fail, we can increase our frequency of success. It sounds simple because it is. The only difficult bit is increasing our consciousness and awareness of these factors in our daily lives. It's my job in this book to make that easy for you.

## A DESIGN FOR LIFE

The whole point of this book is to help you improve your winning record in the game of life, and to target those areas that mean the most to you. This is one crucial area where this book differs from so many others – it aims to leave you with a practical and usable action plan for your life.

At the end of Chapter 1, I am going to ask you to jot down your goals so that you can focus on them while reading on, and add to them as you progress through the book. We're going to work on how to tackle those areas of focus – making use of the lessons in this book

– so that by the time you return to these goals in Chapter 10, you will see a 'before and after' effect.

It's very easy to read a book that is full of good ideas but not implement any of them. Rather than being a book to be passively read and thus largely forgotten about, this will be a manual to be actively learned and used. And don't feel you have to wait until you have finished reading the book before you can implement the techniques – start practising them straight away.

I would encourage you to read with a notebook and pen to hand. I think I can predict how some of you will react to this: 'I can't be bothered to write anything down – it's too much like hard work.' I understand that. However, I would like you to fight against such thoughts for the following compelling reasons.

## WRITING MAKES YOU THINK

It's all too easy to gloss over or skim information. But if you take the time and effort to put pen to paper, you are more likely to think about and to remember what you read.

## WRITING MAKES YOU DO

Drawing up your own bespoke plan helps you to take what is abstract and make it relevant, personal and practical. And that means you are more likely to put the plan into action – action that will produce tangible, winning results.

So, please – give it a try.

This book will then give you the satisfaction of overcoming your weaknesses and achieving what you have always dreamed about but never thought possible. It will give you what will feel like a sneaky advantage over other people because it will equip you with the tools you need to achieve. It's similar to the old Chinese proverb that the charity Oxfam borrowed a few years ago for an advertising campaign:

'Give a man a fish and you may feed him for a day, but teach him how to fish and you may feed him for life.' So I will teach you how to succeed so that where you once failed or made mistakes, you need never do so again. One of my key phrases is: 'Winners make mistakes; they just don't repeat them.'

## The phrase that pays

One way of building yourself up to achieve is to repeat words of encouragement. It may help to have a few easy-to-remember catch-phrases to repeat to yourself as a mantra to aid my winning model of T-CUP: Thinking Correctly Under Pressure. I use such catchphrases several times in this book.

▶ You can change the way you think if you put your mind to it.
▶ Winners make <u>mistakes; they</u> just <u>don't</u> repeat them.
▶ Achieve success from setbacks.
▶ Success doesn't happen in a straight line – it's a learning curve.
▶ Success breeds success when fed on a diet high in self-confidence.
▶ Decode the DNA of success.
▶ You can't excel at everything, but you can always learn, practise and improve at everything.
▶ Winners make their own luck by not leaving anything to chance.
▶ Winners are practical perfectionists: they go for the best result possible.
▶ It's not trial and error; it's trial and refinement.
▶ Winners have 'I will' power.
▶ Shoot for the stars and the sky's the limit. But if you're aimless, you will never hit any targets.
▶ Taking short cuts is a short cut to failure.
▶ Be your personal best.

▶ Experiment in practice; deliver in performance.
▶ Focus on what you can control, not what you can't.
▶ You can only do your best – just make sure you do.
▶ Make a lot of what you've got.
▶ If at first you don't succeed, refine the method. Then try again.
▶ Be autonomous; not an automaton.

# ONE

# WHAT MAKES A WINNER?

## GOALS

☑ to identify the characteristics of a winner
☑ to raise awareness of winning and losing behaviour
☑ to draw up personal target areas to work on throughout this book

## THE UNIVERSAL APPLICATION OF WINNING

Whether you're a mother of three kids or the managing director of three businesses – or indeed both – the basic principles for achieving your desired success are the same. That is because the strategy that all winners use when they succeed is so similar. What follows here is an introduction to the terms I use and a brief outline of the theory that runs through the rest of the book. Once you are familiar with this, you will see how you too can copy and utilise the winning principles in all spheres of your life and begin to enjoy great success.

---

**THINK: What is a winner?**

Before we work out how to become winners, we need to pin down what a winner is in the first place.

1. Take a few moments just to think about what the word 'winner' means to you.
2. Come up with a list of at least five adjectives to describe a winner.
3. Now see if you can sum it up in a sentence, like a dictionary definition.

---

# THE DEFINITION OF A WINNER

I have asked thousands of people for their description of a winner and I always get a different answer. Each dictionary has a slightly different definition; each person has a slightly different interpretation. But most people would accept that winners are people who can 'deliver'.

Over the years of analysing the suitability of job candidates, my company accumulated a database of thousands of people's personal profiles. Though not all of them were necessarily winners, they were all people who had got some way down the line to getting a good job.

Our profiles covered each candidate's personality, mental strengths and weaknesses as well as looking at their intellect. They built up a thorough picture of their overall potential and competence, and their suitability for the job they were applying for. I designed each personal record in such a way that I could get an immediate evaluation of whether or not that person could deliver. I split the database into three very basic categories:

1. Group A – those who would deliver (that is, those with the most potential to succeed)
2. Group B – the mediocre deliverers
3. Group C – the poor deliverers

To find out what set the Group A people apart and why, I sifted out every single trait that characterised them and made them distinct from the others. I wanted to isolate the distinguishing characteristics in Group A that were not possessed by people in the other groups. Read on to find out what these characteristics were.

# WHAT MAKES A WINNER?

Think of someone you know who you would consider to be a winner – preferably someone you know personally rather than someone famous.

Okay, so you've got that person in mind now. Somehow everything seems to go their way, doesn't it? Success seems to come more easily to them for some reason. Why do you think that is? Perhaps you think it's because they are very talented. Or perhaps it's because they're really clever, a right old brain box. Maybe they were just born to be naturally lucky so-and-sos on whom life shines favourably. The truth is, however, that being a winner has little to do with talent, intelligence or luck – as I shall now explain.

## WHAT A WINNER IS NOT...

As I eliminated characteristics when evaluating job candidates, I was able to define a winning deliverer first by what they are – in itself a very useful exercise with surprising results.

### Talent is not crucial

Although I found a lot of talented people in Group A, there were also many talented people in the mediocre and poor groups. This suggested that talent alone was no guarantee of success. We can all think of really talented people who haven't achieved the success they ought to have done for some reason. Equally, we can probably think of some comparatively talentless people who have enjoyed perhaps more than their fair share of success. Look at any reality television show, for example. In life there are always people who 'make a lot of what they've got' and actually make far more than supposedly more talented individuals.

### Intelligence is not crucial

There was no correlation whatsoever between IQ level and being a winner. I found a lot of highly promising people in the other groups. Of course, being clever does not preclude people from being winners, but intelligence alone is not crucial. Indeed, we found several winners who were not overly blessed with intelligence just as we found some highly intelligent people who were certainly not winners. The school geek doesn't always turn out to be top of the class in life.

### Experience is not crucial

Having a lot of experience does not guarantee success. The same goes for having determination or being a hard-worker. We all know people who have been plugging away for ages doing the same old thing and have never made as much progress as they ought to have done. Equally, there are people who come in with no experience and shoot straight to the top.

### AND THE WINNER IS...

So having defined winners by what they are not, I was finally able to define them by what they are. This is the most complete, succinct and accurate definition:

> **A winner is anyone who makes the best use of their personal potential, even when under pressure and/or in competitive situations.**

## TUNE IN TO THE FREQUENCY OF WINNING

I'm not saying that winners never have an off-day; that they succeed all the time. We're all human, not automatons, so we have to allow for an element of human error. And as you will discover, failure is an essential part of the winning process. Just as no one succeeds 100 per cent of the time, so no one fails 100 per cent of the time. Even people who might feel like they always fail sometimes succeed – although they are probably too down on themselves to see it. So we are all capable of maximising our potential from time to time. It's just that we may not experience that winning feeling as often as we would like in order to be self-fulfilled.

The eminent psychologist Abraham Maslow came up with a theory he called the Hierarchy of Needs. His argument was that it is the quest for self-fulfilment that motivates us; that as humans meet 'basic needs', we seek to satisfy successively 'higher needs'. This is what drives us to build on our successes. And that is why our potential to achieve can evolve so that we then have the ability to achieve more and more.

## THE WINNING MODEL

If you want to increase the frequency of your successes and decrease the frequency of your failures, you need not only to meet the 'basic needs' but also to identify the attributes that characterise a winner. This is so that you can work on developing them yourself and become a top performer. For that reason, I have developed the following 'winning model', which I will refer to a lot because it's so universally applicable. It has four important stages, all of which we shall explore in greater depth. By following this winning behaviour model – warrior, thinker, skill refiner, continuous debriefer – you will have the tools, the discipline and the patience to achieve the desired goals you set yourself.

The model is a pyramid that begins with the noble warrior spirit at its base, followed by thinking and finally skill (this goes against the common perception that skill would be the base of winning). Continuous debriefing comes into every stage of the winning model and therefore the diagram shows it running up the side of the pyramid.

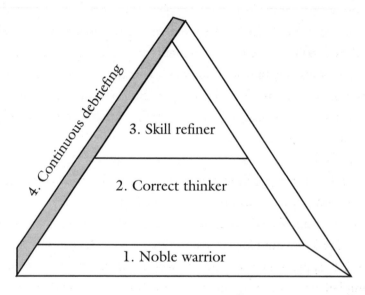

## 1. THE NOBLE WARRIOR

Winners are fighters; not in a physically aggressive sense, but in the sense that they will always face and overcome whatever obstacle or difficulty is in their way – whether it be a heavily bureaucratic system, a driving test or a particularly cantankerous mother-in-law. It is just as important to fight the internal battles – like the devil on your shoulder, the little voice in your head that stops you going for that promotion or approaching that good-looking person at the bar. The noble warrior constantly fights against the self-doubt and negative thoughts that affect all of us from time to time. And the warrior spirit is one that never gives up. It has the discipline and inner strength to go through the mental and physical pain barrier when the going gets tough; to focus on the ultimate goal of success and do everything possible to reach that goal. As such, the noble warrior is the foundation of the winner, underpinning the whole process above it.

## 2. THE CORRECT THINKER

The notion of winning is not unachievable or steeped in mystery. It's based on clear regularity; that's what makes it a formula that can be learned as a skill and repeated. Winners, though they may not even realise it, are driven by the same way of behaving – and that comes foremost from the way they think. Winners think differently to other people. It's not necessarily a more sophisticated way of thinking – sometimes the reverse, in fact – in that it can make some people very focused (think of a champion boxer or an Olympic sprinter). But in all cases it is a very pragmatic way of thinking based on a set of defined do's and don'ts that I am going to teach you.

Fitting within the winning model are 12 winning behaviours that I call T-CUP: Thinking Correctly Under Pressure. (A brief introduction to T-CUP appears below, but we will go through each of the 12 winning behaviours during the course of this book.) Thinking this way is very effective in neutralising the effect of negative thoughts that tend to rear up at critical moments. If we allow negative thoughts to get the better of us, our chances of winning are greatly reduced. The winning formula teaches people how to cope with this, and how to maintain focus and concentration despite unhelpful distraction.

Some people freeze under pressure. Some react on instinct without thinking properly. Others actually perform better as the adrenaline rush of a deadline or a performance brings out the best in them. However, winners are able to perform at their very best whether they are under pressure or not. This is because they train themselves to stay in a thinking mode, no matter what. Winners know that when they are not thinking, they are not in full control of the situation. And if you are not in full control, then your chances of success are vastly reduced.

### 3.THE SKILL REFINER

Winners do not sit back and rest on their laurels. Part of their natural quest for continual and constant improvement is their readiness to practise and polish the skills needed to perform perfectly. But it's a systemised way of improving because you only practise what works. If you practise the winning way, you will see amazing results.

Practising and investing hard work is part of it. The notable success that comes as a result of continually practising the right things with the right attitude may appear to the outside world as innate talent. But, in fact, it is down to putting in the effort and adopting the winning behaviours that this book will teach you.

### 4. CONTINUOUS DEBRIEFING

At each stage, winners are continuously monitoring their performance through a process of debriefing. Traditionally, people only investigate what happened after a failure, to learn the lessons for next time. But by the same logic, we can also learn a great deal from our successes, to deliberately replicate what works. The armed forces debrief after every mission. Winners take it one stage higher: they also debrief during the process to check that they are on the right track at all times. This helps them to correct and adjust their actions in real-time, not just as a result of post-mortem evaluation. This whole process helps to hone the awareness of what works and what doesn't. It helps us to decide on our tactics – whether we should stick with them or change them. And if we need to make changes, it helps us to work out how to do so effectively.

In order to achieve results, winners need to work in an environment that creates a constant sense of competition and challenge. If they exist in a situation where they continually see the results of their colleagues, competitors and even themselves, they feel self-driven to achieve success. It's therefore a characteristic of winners to create an internal, positive and constructive sense of competition that acts as a driver which has the power to lift productivity and therefore achieve results.

This continuous evaluation of performance helps winners to identify how they can increase the frequency of success and decrease the frequency of failure. Debriefing comes naturally to winners because they have a fundamental, self-driven desire to be in a constant state of improvement. Their natural instinct is to ask: 'How could I do this better?' Winners are improving all the time.

The entire winning model is summed up rather nicely in this quote from the philosopher Aristotle:

> *Excellence is an art won by training and habituation. We do not act rightly because we have virtue or excellence, but we rather have those because we have acted rightly. We are what we repeatedly do. Excellence, then, is not an act but a habit.*

## THE WINNING BEHAVIOURS OF T-CUP

Into this basic framework of warrior, thinker, skill refiner and continuous debriefer fit all the winning principles that I have devised. These can be adapted and applied to any sphere of life. Collectively I call these winning behaviours T-CUP, which is short for Thinking

Correctly Under Pressure. Through analysing time and time again precisely what winners do when they succeed, I have isolated the 12 'winning behaviours'. This is a bit like discovering the DNA of success. Now that we have isolated the behavioural process behind success, we can set about replicating it more easily.

As we go through these winning behaviour rules in detail in the chapters that follow, most of them will strike you as just plain common sense do's and don'ts – they are. They are so simple, so easy to remember and so easy to do. And that is precisely the point. Winners are not doing anything especially complicated or difficult when they are winning; just the opposite, in fact – they simplify everything. They are just following common sense – even if they don't realise it. But how much more successful will you be when you realise why you are succeeding?

Here is a taste of what is to come in this book.

## 1. CREATE THE OPPORTUNITY

Fail to prepare and prepare to fail. We know it, yet we ignore it. Why? Because in today's hectic world when we're all rushing around, so many of us feel we don't have time to adequately plan what we are doing. So we will learn the importance and value of spending time and effort preparing and creating the conditions and opportunities necessary to increase the likelihood of success. It's a more refined system of preparation than most people are accustomed to. Less haste, less waste.

## 2. SEIZE THE OPPORTUNITY

Opening the window of opportunity is one thing. Going through it and seizing that opportunity can be quite another. Obstacles and temptations of many sorts can hamper us – such as the temptation to take short cuts. By following the collective principles of T-CUP we will discover how to overcome these obstacles and thus make the most of the opportunities to fulfil our potential. Focus on what you can control, not on what you can't. You can only do your best – just make sure you do.

## 3. MAINTAIN THE MOMENTUM

A winner's persistence helps to perpetuate and preserve accomplishment; to maximise success, minimise failure and continue to improve so that winning is not a sporadic or temporary experience but a continuous and ongoing lifestyle. To this end, we will explore why there is no room for the complacency or overconfidence that often causes people to take short cuts, lose focus or reduce standards after achieving success. We will also look at how to build on success and take the positives from any setbacks we may encounter. Winning is usually not a linear process, and success doesn't happen in a straight line – it's a learning curve. If we learn from the whole experience, the overall pattern will be onwards and upwards. The presence of this learning curve – of winning improvement – is proof of a winner.

## 4. STRIVE FOR THE BEST POSSIBLE RESULT

Winners will not settle for anything less than their best because they know they must be disciplined and conscientious if they want to succeed. We will explore why taking short cuts is normally only a short cut to failure. Success requires patience and thoroughness. Winners strive to be at their best at all times. However, we shall discover why there needs to be a balance between perfectionism and practicality. Winners are practical perfectionists: they go for the best result possible.

## 5. AVOID UNNECESSARY CORNERS

In order to increase the frequency of success, we need to learn how to deliberately avoid unnecessary obstacles that might jeopardise it. This will have the dual benefit of ensuring we won't encounter unnecessary failure so often and of shortening and streamlining our route to success in future. Winners make mistakes; they just don't repeat them. They achieve success from setbacks. We will look at how winners are able to make the most of their skills and their experience; at how they maximise their full potential by simplifying every task they face and learning from their past failures and successes.

## 6. STICK TO WHAT WORKS

There's a lot of truth in the old saying, 'If it ain't broke, don't fix it.' Too often we start messing around needlessly with a winning formula, with unfortunate consequences. So we will look at raising our awareness of winning tactics through a process of continuous debriefing, so we know what we should be sticking to. We'll also learn when we should stick to proven methods and when it is okay to experiment.

## 7. GIVE UP WHAT DOESN'T WORK

We've all heard the phrase, 'If at first you don't succeed, try, try again.' Well that's true up to a point. But if you still don't succeed, it might be time to ask why and then perhaps try a different approach. If at first you don't succeed, refine the method. Then try again. So we will concentrate on how to evaluate what is not working so that we can prune our methods and streamline our path to success. Making mistakes is fine, but only if you learn from them through debriefing. Winning is not trial and error; it's trial and refinement.

## 8. GET BACK TO BASICS

Of course there are going to be times in life when things don't go according to plan. And rather like the driver who gets horribly lost and has to find his or her way back, it can take a long time to return to the right road. But by learning how to get back on track more quickly, we can figure out how to limit any damage.

## 9. IMPROVE YOUR SELF-CONTROL

Winners know how to create their own luck – by controlling as many variables as possible. So we will focus on how we can maintain control by mastering stress and anxiety, and by practising one-step-ahead thinking to ensure we are able to fulfil our potential in any situation. Again, focus on what you can control, not what you can't.

## 10. MAKE THE CORRECT DECISIONS

How do you make the best decision? How do you make any decision at all when none of the options seem right? Some people shy away from life's big decisions through fear of failure or avoidance of discomfort. Others blunder in without thinking things through properly. Improving our decision-making process by evaluating the winning way helps us to arrive at the correct decisions at the right time – thereby helping us to fulfil our potential rather than rue missed opportunities or bad choices.

## 11. LEARN TO THRIVE UNDER PRESSURE

From choking on the pool table black ball to fluffing our lines during a work presentation, many of us freeze when we're under pressure. We shall learn how to fulfil our potential whatever the pressure level, using the principles of T-CUP (Thinking Correctly Under Pressure).

## 12. MAXIMISE YOUR USE OF TIME

We will look at strategies for making the most of our time so that we don't waste it and put ourselves under unnecessary stress. We'll also get into the habit of always taking a moment to think clearly – even when under extreme time pressure – rather than panicking and therefore acting thoughtlessly. Under pressure, you've always got more time than you feel you have.

# PROBLEM PAGES: WHAT ARE YOUR TARGETS?

## THINKING THE WRITE WAY

Look at the headings on the otherwise blank pages that follow (pages 26–29) and spend some time thinking about each of those areas of your life. While doing that, write down on those blank pages under the relevant headings what you would specifically like to improve or work on, and what problems you want to overcome. Be as honest as you can.

Alternatively, take out a big sheet of paper or get a fresh notebook – just make sure you keep what you write down. We will refer back to these notes and add to them as we progress through the book so that by the end you will have created your own bespoke design for life.

Some of you will be tempted to skip this stage and move on to the next chapter. But remember: taking short cuts is normally a short cut to failure. Be a noble warrior and resist that temptation. Remember why:

▶ It will help you **focus** on what you need or want to work on. My experience has shown that people think and concentrate more effectively when asked to put pen to paper.

▶ It will give your reading some **purpose**. The whole idea of this book is that you will address and deal with any areas of your life that you feel could be improved. So these pages will serve as a continuous personal brainstorm that we will add to as we progress through the book, and from which you will discover the solutions to your problems.

▶ It will demonstrate how you can implement the winning behaviours to see **visible improvement** in your own life. Reading is passive; thinking and writing are active.

*Taking the time to define your goals from the start will make you far more likely to achieve them by the end.*

You might write down only one or two things for some categories, and you might jot down 10 for others, but try and come up with at least one target area under each heading. Be as specific or as general as you like at this stage.

Some ideas include:
- ▶ to get a promotion and pay rise at work
- ▶ to save some money for a house
- ▶ to get along better with colleagues
- ▶ to lose a stone
- ▶ to set up your own business
- ▶ to learn how to cook a Sunday roast
- ▶ to learn to hit deadlines
- ▶ to be a better manager
- ▶ to reduce stress
- ▶ to be better accepted by other people
- ▶ to be more daring
- ▶ to develop a level of expertise in your field
- ▶ to have more confidence when you have to cope alone.

Whatever you write down, these are going to be the issues in your life that you will work on and deal with as you read this book. By the time you get to the end, you will be able to come up with a practical and achievable plan to tackle these issues, and you will feel prepared and empowered enough to put that plan successfully into action.

# WHAT'S STOPPING YOU?

You can make the best plans in the world, but unless you act on them, they're not worth the paper they're written on.

It doesn't matter how much talent you have, how much money you have, how clever or lucky you are. The one thing that separates winners from all the rest is drive. Drive to maximise their potential, drive to overcome obstacles, drive to realise their dreams, drive to make life as fulfilling as possible, drive to act on the best-laid plans.

Don't be one of life's plodders, making excuses instead of progress. People who are stuck in a rut feel powerless. They see themselves as victims of circumstance, and they blame other people. This kind of attitude is self-fulfilling defeatism. They don't think they can achieve so they don't.

Winners take responsibility for themselves. They seize control of their destinies, they focus on a goal, and they push themselves towards self-fulfilment. They are bursting with 'I-will' power that propels them over any obstacles.

It's not very British to think this way. But get over that. You are in control, not at the mercy of your culture, your background, your parents, your boss, your company or what your friends think. It's all about you. Be your personal best. Be a little bit selfish and assertive. Not everyone will necessarily be supportive or approve of what you are doing. Do what is best for you, so long as it does not contravene the noble warrior principles. This is how to get ahead in life, so do it. Don't be afraid to be successful – you deserve it and you've earned that right.

The only thing stopping you from being a winner is you. And the sooner you realise that, the sooner you can do something proactive about it. Take control – because no one is just going to give it to you on a plate.

**How can you tell when you are a winner?**

In essence, a winner is someone who frequently displays an upward learning curve of improvement in terms of achieving better and better results in a meaningful area of your life. They don't necessarily have to be perfect or achieve success all the time – that is not practical – but if they are showing continual improvement in their performance level in an area that is meaningful to them, it implies adherence to the winning principles – they are a winner.

## WHERE TO NEXT?

Using proven, practical tools and tips, the following chapters will demonstrate exactly how you can implement the winning model and behaviours in life's key areas – whether they be business, relationships, money, friendships, sport or whatever. By the end of this book, the aim is that you will know how to increase your chances of success and decrease your chances of failure in all areas of life so that you can be a true, self-fulfilled winner. Welcome to the winners' enclosure.

# CAREER, MONEY AND WORK/LIFE BALANCE

# TIME MANAGEMENT, PLANNING AND ORGANISATION

## LOVE, FAMILY AND FRIENDS

WHAT MAKES A WINNER?

# HEALTH, IMAGE AND SELF-ESTEEM

# TWO

# HOW TO DEVELOP A WINNING MINDSET

## GOALS

- ☑ to identify the way in which you think
- ☑ to appreciate the power of positive thinking
- ☑ to develop a winning mindset

## IT'S ALL IN THE MIND

When I was given the rather strange commission to work with the Scottish Institute of Sport Foundation to help change the stereotypically negative attitude of Scottish athletes, I wondered where to begin. How can you go about changing the mindset of a nation? It's not an easy task. But in essence the mindset is the only place to begin. Adopting the right kind of mindset is central to the concept of winning. First, let's have a look at the way you think.

## TO DO: What are you thinking?

What kind of thinker would you say you are generally? An optimist or a pessimist? Maybe you think you're somewhere in between – a realist, perhaps. Or maybe you've never really thought about it.

Read through the following scenarios and the possible reactions to them. Put a tick next to any that you think definitely apply to you, a cross next to any that don't and a question mark alongside any you are not sure about.

**1. I wrote a round-robin email requesting help on a project, but no one replied.**

i)   I'll send it again, stressing the urgency and the value of their contribution.

ii)  How embarrassing – I won't do that again.

iii) Don't know why I bothered – they're all incapable of anything creative.

iv)  They're probably all exchanging round-robin emails about me now.

**2. My taxi got stuck in traffic and I missed my train.**

i)   It's the taxi driver's fault for not knowing a short cut.

ii)  My fault – I should have remembered about the road works.

iii) Why does this always happen to me? I'm useless.

iv)  I'll call and explain and make sure I leave earlier next time.

**3. That person was really nice to me for no reason.**

i)   They probably think I'm a weirdo really.

ii)  What a weirdo.

iii) What a nice person.

iv)  They must fancy me.

**4. An idea I came up with in a meeting was instantly dismissed.**
  i)   I'll think before I speak next time.
  ii)  They wouldn't know a good idea if it smacked them in the face.
  iii) Why do I keep making mistakes?
  iv)  How humiliating – I'll never speak up in a meeting again.

**5. I've lost my keys again.**
  i)   I must put up a key hook right now.
  ii)  It's okay, I bet my housemate has got his keys.
  iii) Today is going to be a bad day, I can tell.
  iv)  I'm always losing everything.

**6. I had a cigarette last night even though I'm trying to quit.**
  i)   It's just too hard to quit.
  ii)  I must tell all my friends not to let me smoke even when I want to.
  iii) I'm pathetic.
  iv)  Why did my friends let me smoke when they know I'm trying to quit?

**7. I'd like to get a pay rise this year.**
  i)   I hope they don't sack me.
  ii)  If I don't get one, I'll quit.
  iii) I bet I don't get one.
  iv)  I'm going to ask the boss what I need to do to get one.

**8. I got turned down for a bank loan.**
  i)   The other bank will probably give me double anyway.
  ii)  I'll never have any money!
  iii) I'll improve my application and try again.
  iv)  I knew they'd turn me down.

**9. I'd like to ask a friend at work out on a date.**

   i)   I'll ask them what kinds of things they're interested in.

   ii)  What if they say no?

   iii) I hope it doesn't make everyone else jealous.

   iv) As if they'd want to go out with me!

**10. I'd like to do some more exercise.**

   i)   It's not my fault I am big-boned and have a slow metabolism.

   ii)  But I'm far too embarrassed to exercise in public.

   iii) I wonder if my friend would come running with me.

   iv) I've tried going to the gym before and it never works.

Later in the chapter (page 40) we'll analyse your answers.

## THE OPTIMIST, THE PESSIMIST AND THE REALIST

The way we look at life and every situation it presents has a huge influence on how we feel and therefore on our ability to achieve and succeed. Although there will always be some blurring of the lines depending on the situation and which side of bed we got out of that morning, we should broadly fit in to one of the following four categories:

1. The typical pessimist
2. The worst-case pessimist
3. The winning optimist
4. The naive optimist

### The naive optimist versus the winning optimist

The winning mindset is an optimistic mindset. However, it might surprise you to learn that not all optimism is desirable or beneficial.

When optimism is misplaced, it can be just as dangerous as pessimism. This kind of optimism we shall call 'naive optimism'.

## 1. Chance
▶ A naive optimist can be the king (or queen) of wishful thinking, relying too much on fate or luck for success. 'I'm sure it'll be fine... I've got a good feeling...'
▶ A winning optimist puts in the effort to ensure that nothing is left to chance. 'Have we considered every possibility? Let's form a contingency plan...'

## 2. Problem-solving
▶ A naive optimist may ignore problems or blame them on others rather than face up to them, assuming they will just go away or that they will be able to deal with them. The result is that small problems can often escalate into major issues. 'I'm sure we don't really need that permit... Forget about that for now... We'll come back to that later... Just make do with that for now.' In their naivety, they might just not foresee any problems and so not account for them.
▶ A winning optimist will operate on a 'stitch in time saves nine' basis and ensure that all problems are dealt with as they arise so that they don't snowball into big issues. 'Let's sort this out now...' They will accept responsibility where appropriate and take affirmative action to remedy any problems, including ones that others have not foreseen.

## 3. Responsibility
▶ A naive optimist might well avoid responsibility whenever anything goes wrong. External factors are always to blame; nothing is ever their fault. 'They haven't got a clue... If he

hadn't done that then this wouldn't have happened... They ought to have thought of that...'

▶ A winning optimist knows when to accept responsibility (but won't claim it unnecessarily as a pessimist might). 'Fair enough, I'll take that advice on board for next time...'

## 4. Credit

▶ A naive optimist will often be only too happy to see success as further confirmation of their greatness or good fortune. This can come across as distastefully conceited or smug. 'I knew I'd win... I never had any doubt... Would you expect anything else!'

▶ A winning optimist knows when to accept credit and how to enjoy success but will often reflect glory on to others and share it out. 'We couldn't have done it without the great team we have behind us...'

## 5. Assumption

▶ A naive optimist will often assume they know what's best for other people and will plough on regardless, even if they get it wrong. 'Trust me, you'll see... I thought that's what you wanted...'

▶ A winning optimist will always check that people know what is happening to make sure everything is on track. 'Can I just check you're happy with this?'

## 6. Learning

▶ A naive optimist will not think to debrief continuously because they are confident they will do everything just fine time and time again. 'No worries...'

▶ A winning optimist knows the value of learning from both failures and successes so that the former can be edited out and the latter replicated. 'How could we do that better? Next time, let's remember x, y and z.'

## The problem with pessimists

Pessimists are more likely to be right than optimists but are less likely to succeed. Optimists (especially naive ones) tend to overestimate the positive and think things are much better than they actually are, whereas pessimists may have a more realistic and therefore accurate idea. However, optimists have more success because they try harder to attain the success they predicted. Pessimists, when they are proved 'right' by failure, operate a 'told-you-so' policy and stop there. Just as optimists contribute to their success with a positive mindset, there is a danger that a pessimistic opinion can also be a self-fulfilling one. Pessimists are so determined to maintain their negative opinion that they will go out of their way to prove it is correct, even if they suffer as a result. It's like cutting off their nose not just to spite their face, but to prove that it is ugly as well.

When you think positively, you will feel more in control, and you will believe that you will find a solution. Without even realising it, you mobilise all your senses and systems to bring about success. 'I can make it… We can do this… Let's give it our best shot…'

Think negatively, and you won't feel so in control or capable of finding solutions. Indeed, your senses and systems work against you to scupper your progress. 'I can't do it… We're not going to make it… What's the point?'

There are gradations of pessimist. We normally only think of the doom-mongers as pessimists. However, many so-called 'realists' actually have pessimistic tendencies that need to change. This kind of attitude is fairly common and underpins a lot of widespread cynicism and sarcasm. Here are some of the classic characteristics of pessimism to watch out for:

## 1. Exaggeration

Pessimists often overstate the negative elements of a situation while ignoring or understating any positive aspects. 'It's a complete and utter disaster. The whole thing is ruined!'

## 2. Problem-solving

Pessimists will often find that small problems quickly get blown out of all proportion and render the whole situation impossible to the point where they give up completely. 'Why does everything always go wrong?'

## 3. Responsibility

Pessimists often assume that if something goes wrong it's because of them (either consciously or unconsciously) and so they are very quick to blame themselves. 'I'm so sorry, it must all be my fault…' Or they are very quick to go on the extreme defensive for the purposes of self-preservation. 'What are you looking at me for? I didn't do it.'

## 4. Credit

Pessimists often assume that if something goes right it's in spite of them and will attribute credit elsewhere. 'It was nothing to do with me – thank her!'

## 5. Assumption

Pessimists might assume the worst on behalf of others without any solid evidence to back it up. 'I bet they hate me now…'

## 6. Learning

Pessimists don't debrief properly either, taking the view that 'what will be, will be'. Failures will be seen as expected confirmation of their inabilities. 'I knew that would happen.' Successes are seen as unexpected flukes. 'I bet I couldn't do that again if I tried.' In neither case are the appropriate lessons learned for the future.

## Get realist

If men are from Mars and women are from Venus, then what planet are optimists on? Some people think optimists live in cloud cuckoo land; that they expect way too much and that in reality things will never live up to those expectations. Many people won't pigeonhole themselves as pessimists with all the negative connotations that entails. Instead they see themselves as realists, people who see things as they really are, without a falsely negative or positive spin on them.

A realist will argue that by being realistic, they will never expect too much. And if you don't expect much, you won't ever be disappointed. Sorry to disappoint you realists, but that is untrue.

Say, for example, a winning optimist, a pessimist and a realist all see a great job in the paper that they would love to have, but might be just beyond their current experience level. A pessimist wouldn't even bother going for it. The realist and the winning optimist will both give it their best shot but when neither of them gets it, the realist will say, 'Thought as much – oh well, I'm glad I didn't get my hopes up too much.' And at that point they will stop.

The winning optimist, being optimistic, will typically see the positive side. Feeling disappointed is not in their nature – at least not for long. They would start by debriefing. They might think: 'That was a good experience; I now know what to do better next time. I'll get some feedback, research this area a bit more and try again.' No prizes for guessing who gets the most success. That's the reality.

## TO DO: What kind of thinker are you?

Go back to the questionnaire options on page 32 and see if you agree with the key below. (The key is correct by the way.)

A = The winning optimist
B = The typical pessimist
C = The naive optimist
D = The worst-case pessimist

1.  i) = A    ii) = B    iii) = C    iv) = D
2.  i) = C    ii) = B    iii) = D    iv) = A
3.  i) = D    ii) = B    iii) = A    iv) = C
4.  i) = A    ii) = C    iii) = B    iv) = D
5.  i) = A    ii) = C    iii) = B    iv) = D
6.  i) = B    ii) = A    iii) = D    iv) = C
7.  i) = D    ii) = C    iii) = B    iv) = A
8.  i) = C    ii) = D    iii) = A    iv) = B
9.  i) = A    ii) = B    iii) = C    iv) = D
10. i) = C    ii) = D    iii) = A    iv) = B

Now add up the number of ticks, crosses and question marks you have for each letter.

|  | TICKS | CROSSES | QUESTION MARKS |
|---|---|---|---|
| A. Winning optimist | | | |
| B. Typical pessimist | | | |
| C. Naive optimist | | | |
| D. Worst-case pessimist | | | |

To be a winning optimist, you'll need to have the most ticks in category A. If you have, that's great. You already have a winning mindset that will help you implement the advice and tools in the rest of this book. If your total for category C is greater than your total for category A, then you probably need to look at managing your optimism a little better, in line with the winning formula. If you scored highly in categories B and D, then we will need to work on boosting your powers of positive thought.

Whatever your score, it is always possible to hone your sense of winning optimism. It's not a revolution; it's a gradual process. And it starts now.

# THE WINNING MINDSET

The way you think strongly determines what kind of mindset you have. The good news is that you can change the way you think. Some people are concerned that changing their mindset is a difficult task. What many don't realise is that it is something we do every day. If you are due to have an operation you will be initially worried and afraid, but you then accept that it is for the best and will mean you recover more quickly: this is an example of changing your mindset. When a child does something unintentionally dangerous, the parent's first instinct is to be angry, but they then control their emotions and calmly explain to the child what was wrong: again, this is changing one's mindset.

Winners need an open mind, one that is receptive to new ideas and thinking differently. That's not to say they need accept all ideas – an open mind is still a working mind. Winners and losers may see the same opportunities but it is the way they view these opportunities that makes them different. Just be prepared to give things a try.

## THE LOSER'S MINDSET

Having a loser's mindset doesn't need to be as obvious as thinking, 'I'm a complete failure, I can't do anything and the world is against me.' Thankfully, very few of us are that desperately pessimistic, except for when we're having a really bad day. The loser's mindset is actually a bit more insidious and might disguise itself as the mindset of a realist or a fatalist – 'what will be, will be'. It's like having the devil on our shoulder, constantly chipping away at our confidence bit by bit, undermining our ability to fulfil our potential, and keeping us pegged down.

Those of the loser's mindset believe that talents and abilities are set in stone at birth or during childhood – you either have them or you don't. So they might adopt the Homer Simpson school of thought: 'Trying is the first step to failure.' This leads to nowhere. Any failure is taken to be a 'told you so' reinforcement of their negative view. Thinking otherwise, they believe, will lead only to disappointment. Successes are played down and attributed to luck or someone else, seen as an aberration rather than the norm.

People who think in this way tend not to feel in complete control of their lives. They feel they are controlled by others or by the systems and culture in which they work. Psychologists refer to this as having an 'external locus of control'. This is quite a common British mindset, thanks to a hangover from the class system and strictly enforced hierarchies. Its effect is to stunt development, thereby inhibiting success.

## THE WINNER'S MINDSET

Having a winner's mindset doesn't necessarily mean going round telling everyone you're the best thing since sliced bread. Thankfully, very few of us are like that. But as with the loser's mindset, there is a drip-drip process at work. It's like having an angel on our shoulder who keeps whispering encouragement in our ear, telling us we can do it, pushing us to have a go and make the most of our opportunities.

Those of a winner's mindset believe that potential is not a finite product, that talents can be developed and that great abilities are built over time. In other words, stars can be made as well as born. You can achieve if you want to; you can maximise your potential if you put your mind to it. This leads to improvement: increased frequency of success and decreased frequency of failure. The approach is more optimistic: failure is chalked up to experience, something to be learned from, because 'winning doesn't happen in a straight line'. Failure is also seen as an aberration rather than the norm. Success is seen as confirmation that everything is on the right track rather than as a stroke of luck.

| LOSER'S MINDSET LANGUAGE | WINNER'S MINDSET LANGUAGE |
|---|---|
| That's the way we've always done things around here | Is there a better, newer way of doing things? |
| Know your place – don't get ideas above your station | Create opportunities and make the most of them |
| I'm not cut out for this | I can do this |
| That'll do | How can I improve? |
| Be realistic: don't waste your time | Be realistic, but let's give it a go |
| No chance | It's worth a try |
| Why? | Why not? |

People who think in this way tend to feel more in control of their lives and their destinies. They are not dictated to by circumstance or by other people. They are active rather than passive and as such have what psychologists call an 'internal locus of control'.

Anthropological studies suggest that this mindset is more common in comparatively new countries and cultures, such as America and Australia, where there is less history of enforced hierarchies.

## CAN YOU CHANGE YOUR MIND AND BECOME A WINNER?

Of course all this is a necessary simplification of the complicated workings of the human mind. And many of us will probably go through stages of both mindsets, depending on our mood, our level of self-confidence and a whole host of other variables. However, all of us will tend more to one side than the other.

So can you change?

Those of a loser's mindset will say you can't – of course, they would. That's one of their characteristics. They are stuck in their ways, bound by their culture, restricted to the way they have been brought up and taught. Likewise, those of a winner's mindset will say you can – you are in control of your life so you can decide what you do and don't do, what you think and don't think.

Happily, the experts are siding with the winners. Personality psychologists – such as Dr Carol Dweck, the world authority in this area – now believe that the winner's mindset can be both taught and caught (that is, socialised) in all spheres of life.

Early academic thinking suggested that we were not able to choose how we think; that we were a product both of genetics and how we were brought up in our so-called 'formative years'. Most people think that once we get set in our ways, that's it: 'You can't teach an old dog new tricks.' Thinking this way restricts us from fulfilling our potential – which is central to winning. Our formative years actually never end. We can change the way we think whenever we want. Like now.

## BE AUTONOMOUS, NOT AN AUTOMATON

We tend to underestimate how much of our personality is changeable if we want it to be. That's not to say we all need to become the same person and try to force-fit ourselves into a set template. It just means that we don't need to revert to our default settings all the time if we don't want to, especially if those settings are inhibiting our ability to reach our potential and be winners.

Simply changing your mindset might sound obvious, but it's remarkable how few people do it. Having a pessimistic, negative mindset is not helpful or productive, so there's little point thinking like that. If you can change the way you see things so that you are a more optimistic and positive person, you will be happier and more popular as well as more successful. Negative people are energy and enthusiasm sappers; positive people are naturally nicer to be around.

The winning mindset will not come overnight, but the more you work at it, the more natural it will feel. It's like learning to drive. To start with all you can think is mirror-signal-manoeuvre-don't-knock-over-that-old-lady. But after a bit of practice, everything clicks and it all feels like second nature. Stick with it. You can change the way you think if you put your mind to it.

# THE POWER OF POSITIVE THINKING

Changing the way you think will help you overcome nerves and pressure as well as negativity and self-doubt. Like drinking a can of emotional Red Bull, it gives you a little pick-me-up when you need some get-up-and-go attitude. The more you experience success from positive thinking, the more you will trust in its power. But to realise that, you need to give it a go. So try this:

## SEE NO EVIL

The word 'visualisation' might sound a bit airy-fairy, like the 'psychobabble' you find in self-help books. The truth is that we visualise all the time – when we 'imagine the worst-case scenario' or 'hope for the best'. So we may as well learn how to harness the power of visualisation to help us rather than allow it to hinder us. If we allow negative thoughts to get the better of us, we'll be too scared to try anything, trapped by a crippling fear of failure. But if we can picture success, immediately our frown softens, the tension in our shoulders eases and a smile may even appear. Visual images are hugely powerful: this is why video montages of success (usually set to music) are so inspiring in the worlds of sport and business. Visualise achieving your goal; visualise how you are going to achieve it practically, step by step; visualise coping well with any nerves and pressure; visualise what it will feel like, how you will feel afterwards, what effect it will have. Simulators are used to train pilots and surgeons so that they know how to respond in real-life situations. So simulate for your own purposes: how that meeting with your boss will work out when you ask for a promotion, or how your speech will go, or how that big match is going to pan out. Automatically, you will feel more ready to take the bull by the horns and go for it. Approaching anything with that kind of attitude is far more likely to bring about a positive result than being timid or afraid – or worse still, not trying at all.

## HEAR NO EVIL

You have to silence your critics – literally. If people around you are constantly undermining your confidence by telling you or making you feel like you're no good, you need to get away from them. Don't weigh yourself down with negativity – it's very exhausting after a while. Instead, keep yourself buoyed by positive influences. Draw strength and encouragement from supportive people. This is why team-talks, motivational speeches and crowd support can be so powerful. It's also why people like to psyche themselves up with rousing music.

## SPEAK NO EVIL

The other critic you need to silence is the one inside your head, the little devil on your shoulder who keeps filling you with self-doubt. This is where 'self-talk' comes into play. Be a scriptwriter for the little angel on your other shoulder. Give them ammunition to shout down the little devil. Gee yourself up with words of encouragement. 'Come on! I can do it! Can't wait! Let's go! I'll show them...' and so on. I like to use helpful and memorable catchphrases such as those you'll find in the Introduction on page 7.

## TO DO: Feel the force of change

Think of something you have to do in the next few days that you are not much looking forward to. It doesn't matter what it is or how mundane – attending a big board meeting, doing the weekly food shop or putting up with the in-laws for dinner...

Now force yourself to think about it more positively. You're full of boundless enthusiasm for the task; you can't wait till it starts; you're going to thoroughly enjoy it; it will bring lots of benefits. Feel faintly ridiculous? Okay, but it's better than feeling full of dread. Simply by choosing to think about the task differently, you can completely alter the experience for the better.

Of course, it's much easier to think positively if you are full of confidence and self-belief. That's the subject of the next chapter.

# THREE

# HOW TO IMPROVE YOUR SELF-BELIEF

## GOALS

☑ to recognise the strong relationship between mindset and winning
☑ to measure your confidence level so that you can build on it
☑ to overcome any fear of failure and problems of low self-confidence
☑ to increase your self-belief so that you can achieve

## TO DO: How does this make you feel?

Put yourself in the following hypothetical situations and try to rate your likely confidence level with a score of 0–10 (0 = zero confidence and 10 = brimming with confidence).

| HYPOTHETICAL SITUATION | CONFIDENCE LEVEL (0–10) |
|---|---|
| 1. Your boss criticises a project you have been managing. | |
| 2. You have 10 minutes to prepare a joke to tell in front of 100 people. | |
| 3. At a restaurant, your partner's meal is undercooked and you want to complain. | |
| 4. You come quite low down in an office poll of the most attractive person. | |
| 5. Your work conference is at a beach resort and everyone has been told to bring their swimming costume. | |
| 6. You're playing mixed doubles and are about to serve for the match. | |
| 7. A colleague spreads an embarrassing rumour about you around the company. | |
| 8. You've got to go to hospital to have some blood tests done. | |
| 9. On your late-night walk home, you spot a gang of teenage lads coming towards you. | |
| 10. It's your first day in a completely new job. | |

Add your scores up.

**Less than 40** = You really need to work on boosting your confidence all round in order to feel like a winner. This chapter is going to be very useful for you.

**40–60** = There are certainly situations where you feel low on confidence. Make a note of them on your 'problem pages' in Chapter 1 and use the advice in this chapter to target those particular areas.

**61–80** = Your confidence level seems to be pretty good. Is it always like this or are there days when you feel low on confidence? Are there any areas of your life where you wish you had more belief in yourself? If we're honest, most of us do – winners included.

**81+** = Confidence doesn't seem to be a problem for you. But overconfidence might be. Has anyone ever accused you of being overconfident? Is your confidence ever misplaced? And is your confidence genuine? If you feel truly satisfied with your level of confidence, then perhaps you should move on to the next chapter.

## ARE YOU A BELIEVER?

Whether they are the managing director of a big company, a lightning-quick 100m sprinter or a gangster rapper, successful people all have certain things in common that help them succeed: competitive drive and a strong belief in their right to be on the winning side. Some of them might try and hide it (although probably not the rapper) but it's there. Or – and this is the key – at least that is the attitude they project. Think for a moment about some successful people you know in your own life and you'll find it's true.

However, the fact is that all of us – no matter whether we are at the top of the tree or the bottom of the pile – suffer from a crisis of confidence at various points. Clearly, some people are naturally more confident than others, but each and every one of us could do with improving our levels of self-belief. And that is what this chapter is all about.

## HOW TO INCREASE YOUR SELF-BELIEF

Now that we have started to work on developing a winning mindset, we can move on to the next stage: building up self-belief. The two things are intertwined and feed off each other: once you are thinking more positively, you are prepared to give things a proper go and so you achieve more. The more you accumulate positive winning experience, the easier it is to develop self-belief, and once you believe in yourself, the more optimistic you will be.

In order to experience winning on purpose and on a frequent basis rather than as what you might perceive to be an occasional 'fluke', you first need to feel like a winner. Until we've got our heads in the right place, we can do nothing. We cannot expect to run a winning way of life, and enjoy doing so, if we don't have the initial self-belief that we can do it – and that we deserve it. If a rock star goes on stage when he's not in the mood to perform, the crowd will hate him. If you go into a job interview thinking you haven't got a hope, you will come across badly to the interviewer and you'll be very unlikely to get the job.

The good news is that, if you can boost your self-belief the winning way, then you will notice a significant increase in your success rate. Nothing influences your self-belief more than winning. Success breeds success when it is fed by high self-confidence.

## THE POWER OF FEELINGS

Feelings are hugely powerful. As we've already touched on, they dictate our mood and thus affect both our ability and our willingness to do anything. If we are feeling negative, then we are less likely to think of solutions, and our ability to achieve and our willingness to have a go are markedly reduced. In contrast, if we are feeling positive, then our ability to come up with solutions and to achieve – and our willingness to have a go – increase significantly.

Imagine how the same scenario can be affected by your confidence level. Jane and Megan have just returned from holiday together and are due to go to their friend Andrea's birthday drinks party. Jane is feeling run-down after travelling and wakes up with post-holiday blues and a nasty spot emerging on her chin. She just doesn't feel like facing people. So she calls Megan and makes an excuse not to go, and then spends the evening feeling miserable and guilty for not making the effort.

Megan feels fantastically rested after a week on the beach and has a great tan that she can't wait to show off at the party. Full of confidence, she is the life and soul of the party and ends up meeting John who is now her boyfriend.

Some people feel like utter failures all the time. Some people feel like they can take on the world every day. The reality is that most people fit somewhere between the two but will experience both extremes – and something as trivial as feeling a bit worn-out can dictate which one.

If your default settings tend to be quite negative because of low self-belief, then we need to work on boosting you up. Often all it takes is to realise the futility of thinking negatively, and to force yourself to think more positively – as the exercise in the last chapter demonstrated (see page 47). However, you can't make that change effective if you don't believe in it. There is only one person you will never be able to fool – and that person is yourself. So we have to convince you to be more positive.

No one finds it easy to go against their natural instinct. It is by definition unnatural to do so. This means that for someone who often feels like a failure, feeling like a winner and experiencing the joy and satisfaction of success might feel strange and quite alien – even undeserved. And these feelings are often reinforced by those around us who want to exert their power, or undermine ours. Life – especially at work and other competitive areas – is unfortunately often full of people who would like to put us down. The effect of this might be that we end up putting ourselves down. This means that through a lack of self-belief, we won't give things a go. That is a huge restriction on our ability to maximise our potential and thus experience winning on a regular basis. It's a restriction we must overcome.

A massive pre-requisite for being a winner is developing the unwavering belief that we deserve it, that we are entitled to succeed, that it is worth having a go – whatever anyone else or our own self-doubt might say to the contrary.

The truth is that the person who feels like a failure will succeed sometimes, even if they are too low on self-confidence to admit it. For them, the success makes little lasting impact on how they feel. By the same token, the person who feels invincible will fail every now and then, even if they are so full of self-confidence that the failure barely even registers. So for them, the setback does not throw them off course or slow their momentum. The key difference here is the level of self-belief. So to be a winner, you must maintain a high level of self-belief.

## KEEP A SENSE OF PERSPECTIVE

You can feel confident in some areas of your life and unconfident in others. Just as confidence can spread from one part of your life to others so the reverse is true – often with catastrophic effects. Sometimes feeling 'useless' in just one area of your life that means a great deal to you can infect other parts and make you feel like a failure as a person. For example:

▶ Someone who struggles with mathematics may feel that they are 'thick' even if they are in fact quite gifted in other areas.

▶ Someone who has been passed over for promotion twice might have zero confidence at work and be devoid of any ambition or enthusiasm.

▶ Someone who hasn't had a partner in a long time might feel like they will never have one, and that makes them feel very down about life in general.

▶ For someone else, being overweight might seriously blight all parts of their life.

One issue becomes all-pervading and snowballs. If we feel low for long enough, it becomes a state of mind. If it stays as a state of mind for long enough, then it becomes our identity. It doesn't need to be like this. Feeling low is a subjective state of mind. The winner's response is to get some objective perspective; to try and see it from a different angle, a more balanced one. How? By reminding yourself of all the other meaningful successes that you have chosen to forget about in order to dwell on one failing.

Feeling (subjectively) useless in an important area of your life doesn't necessarily mean that you actually are (objectively) useless in that area. And of course it certainly doesn't mean that you are useless altogether. Life rarely works to the binary scale of good or bad, success or failure. The likelihood is that you are not a complete zero, but that you could improve. Try not to think in all-or-nothing terms, but rather award yourself a percentage of success that you can look to improve upon. Winners approach life in this regard: 'You can't excel in everything but you can always learn, practise and improve anything you touch!' If you repeat that to yourself like a mantra and live it out, your self-perception will change.

We all have different gifts. You might not yet be a master of the areas of your life that are most important to you – which you noted down at the end of Chapter 1 – but there will be areas of your life that you place less importance on in which you are very successful. It's important to remember these and enjoy them too.

## TO DO: On your marks

1. Refer back to the areas of your life you would like to feel more positive about (see the 'problem pages' in Chapter 1). As objectively as you can, award yourself a percentage mark to represent how positive you currently feel about each of these areas: for example, 0 = utter despair, 50 = average, and so on. Write these marks down along with the date. You can refer back to and update these marks as we go through the book, as indicated in the sample table below, to see if you feel they are improving. And if not, you need to keep plugging away at developing a more positive, winning mindset. It's important to keep these practical targets in focus, and to try and see a sense of measurable progression.

| TARGET AREA | POSITIVITY % DATE: 15 Mar | POSITIVITY % DATE: 15 Apr | POSITIVITY % DATE: | POSITIVITY % DATE: | POSITIVITY % DATE: |
|---|---|---|---|---|---|
| Career progression | 30 | 40 | | | |
| Timekeeping | 40 | 60 | | | |
| Relationship with father | 15 | 25 | | | |
| Etc. | Etc. | Etc. | | | |

2. A healthy mindset is all about balance. With that in mind, now think of at least two things you are good at and a list of reasons why you are good at them. Note them down if you want to. Make a plan today to go and do those things this week. If you're good at giving presentations, then arrange to give one. If you're a great parent, then book something fun for you to do as a family this week. It's important for a sense of perspective that you enjoy the feeling of being good at things, rather than focusing solely on those areas that need improvement.

# BOOSTING YOUR SELF-RESPECT

It's one of life's truisms that people respect those who respect themselves, and people treat you the way you treat yourself. If you don't respect yourself, other people will not respect you either. If you don't feel, look and act like a winner, you will not be treated as one.

Think of it in simple terms: people who don't care about themselves might not make an effort to look nice or to speak to people. Perhaps they were not part of the 'in' crowd at school and so got bullied. Perhaps they don't feel valued or appreciated at home by their partner or at work by their boss. People get so used to being downtrodden that they come to expect it.

But if you look and act the part and put yourself across as someone who is confident and happy, then you will behave differently and so people will treat you with more respect. Even something as simple as a new haircut can do wonders for your self-confidence. That's why there are so many makeover shows on television. The right amount of self-confidence is attractive.

Body language and tone of voice are also important:

▶ Look people in the eye, don't look down or away.
▶ Smile and laugh, don't frown or look worried.
▶ Hold your head up high, pull your shoulders back and walk with confidence rather than slumping in your chair or shuffling when you walk.
▶ Convey enthusiasm, not boredom, in your voice.

Being a shiny, happy person might perhaps go against your natural character, maybe even your culture. Many people in Britain are famously cynical and their language is heavily influenced by sarcasm. That's fine up to a point: the point at which the cynicism and negativity begin to infect and negatively influence their personality. If you think and say something negative often enough, you begin to believe it.

Compare this with the stereotype of Americans and Australians who come across as more self-confident. It's a national stereotype because that is how they seem to project themselves to the rest of the world. Taken to the nth degree, of course, this can go too far the other way and come across as overconfidence, arrogance or self-obsession. Once it crosses that line, people lose respect for you once again, so it's important to strike a balance.

The important thing to bear in mind is that people don't automatically give you respect. You have to be a noble warrior and go and get it. The noble warrior is the foundation level of the winning behaviour model (see page 14). It is about being proactive in fighting against any obstacle to success, whether it be external or internal. You have to break out of the vicious circle that perpetuates negativity and low self-worth.

That means you may have to toughen up. Speak up, stand up for yourself, be assertive. Do not accept or tolerate disrespect towards you because as soon as you start to put up with it, you're on the slippery slope to the bottom of the pile where you will be trodden on.

So how do you earn respect? Not by being brutal, dishonest or inconsiderate. That's not earning respect like a noble warrior; that is trying to force it. Let's look at an example.

---

## THINK: When respect is due

1. Take a few moments to think about someone you respect and admire, preferably someone you know personally as opposed to a famous person.
2. Why do you respect them?
3. Can you list their qualities?
4. Add any qualities that you would like to work on yourself to your personal 'problem pages' in Chapter 1.

---

## The vicious and the virtuous circles

**Vicious:** Low self-confidence breeds lower self-confidence and feeds off feelings of negativity (such as failure, defensiveness, pessimism, cynicism).

**Virtuous:** High self-confidence breeds higher self-confidence and feeds off feelings of positivism (such as success, openness, optimism).

---

# THE CONFIDENCE SEESAW

Your self-confidence is the balance between your accumulated positive experiences (your successes) to date versus the negative ones (your failures). So each failure potentially has a negative impact on your self-confidence. The scale of that impact depends on how meaningful the failure is on your confidence seesaw. The more weight you have on the positive side, the less impact a negative experience will have. The more weight you have on the negative side, the less impact a positive experience will have. Put simply, you need more weight on the positive side in order to absorb any negative impact without being tipped the other way.

Creating and maintaining the weight on the positive side is the challenge. This means you have to apply the winning behaviours of T-CUP (see page 17) to:

▶ significantly reduce and minimise experiences and feelings of failure
▶ significantly improve and enhance experiences and feelings of success
▶ give yourself credit when you do achieve rather than allowing yourself to wallow in negativity.

Only when you have created the right frame of mind are you at a stage where you can fulfil your true potential and become a winner. This is something you can work on while winning – and of course it will come more easily the more success you have – but you have to make it happen to begin with by following the winning behaviour model. Just follow that and act accordingly and you will significantly increase your success rate and therefore your self-belief. Start by being a warrior and push yourself to keep going when you get to the stage where you would normally give up.

## HOW TO OVERCOME A FEAR OF FAILURE: INCREASE YOUR 'I WILL' POWER

Generally speaking, we're not a terribly adventurous lot by nature. There is an all-pervading fear of failure, fear of the unknown and reluctance to change the status quo. This is very limiting and restrictive, inhibiting our winning potential. It means that we are often reluctant to make decisions in the first place, and when we do make them, they tend not to be as proactive as they could be.

When feeling low on confidence, our natural tendency is to shy away from any situation in which we might have to do something. And we will find excuses in our heads to support our decision to evade confronting the situation. We naturally want to sneak away from additional proof as to our 'failings' and thus make ourselves feel less bad. The reality is that this doesn't work – we'll resent ourselves for being pathetic, for not giving things a go. We'll go to such great lengths to avoid having to confront the situation that it will become exhausting. By avoiding situations because of a fear of failure, our mind is unconsciously marking down our behaviour as a failure anyway.

When we see someone who has tried and failed – perhaps a friend who tried to set up her own business, or a colleague who left the company but didn't like his new job – we see this as evidence that we should stick with what we've got: better the devil you know than the devil you don't. But the fact is that more of us say 'if only I had' rather than 'I wish I hadn't'. For every person who is a bit impetuous and rushes in without thinking things through properly, there are many more who haven't the courage to act on their dreams, to give things a try, and who live with that regret forever. Winners act in a way that maximises the potential for success: they don't rush in without thinking, but nor do they spend forever dreaming and never doing.

It's not like there is a particularly amazing secret to success. Again, a lot of it boils down to self-belief, as a theory called the Pygmalion Effect suggests. The theory goes that one of the main reasons why successful and decisive people are successful and decisive is because they believe they are successful and decisive in the way they implement the winning model.

Similarly, one of the main reasons that unsuccessful and indecisive people are unsuccessful and indecisive is because they believe they are unsuccessful and indecisive. In both cases, the power of self-belief makes it a self-fulfilling prophecy. Be proactive and make decisions and you're on your way to being a winner. And don't worry when you make mistakes. It's normal – winners make mistakes too. It's just that they learn from them for future reference, thus turning a negative into a positive.

## TALK YOURSELF INTO IT

Psychologists swear by the power of self-talk. So instead of saying 'I can't', say 'I can' and 'I will.' Return to the big decision you have to make. Now say to yourself: 'I will do it.' And believe it. Don't leave it up to fate. Don't worry about what might go wrong. Just do whatever it takes to achieve it. Boost your 'I will' power and automatically your mindset will become a winning mindset.

Making proactive and positive decisions can help us:

▶ beat the fear of failure and of the unknown
▶ break away from the restrictive status quo
▶ reduce our sense of powerlessness
▶ reduce our feelings of regret and 'if only'
▶ maximise our winning potential.

Being a winner is not just about making the opportunities, but about taking them too. There may be a few ups and downs along the way. That's natural: winning doesn't happen in a straight line. Just don't stop where others stop because of poor self-belief or self-discipline. Be a warrior and fight back against any setbacks and obstacles. Take control of your life and you will feel more empowered, more proactive, less stressed and more likely to achieve your goals. The decision is yours.

## How to feel like a winner

▶ Live in the now – to be able to enjoy your achievements, you've got to be aware of them to begin with. So you need to give yourself credit when you succeed.

▶ Don't live only in the past – either by dwelling on past failures or harping back to the good old times too much.

▶ Don't live only in the future – if you're always looking to the next step, always worrying about tomorrow's problems, your life will slip away without your being able to consciously enjoy it. Many people miss out on the enjoyment in an effort to keep chasing the next success, and that is why they are never happy. Live for the moment and in the moment.

## WHY BUILDING CONFIDENCE HELPS IN DEALING WITH PROBLEMS

The problem with problems is that they always crop up; there are always new ones. But the more confident you are in your ability to overcome and solve problems, the less stressed you will feel about them, and the less problematic they will be. So building confidence helps to boost your problem immune system. The less confident you are, the more likely it is that relatively minor problems will strike you down. If you can nip problems in the bud, they will not escalate to become hugely stressful situations that could take their toll on your health and/or personal life. You will be free of trouble and you will sleep better!

## HOW TO IMPROVE YOUR SUCCESS RATE
## WHEN CONFIDENCE IS LOW

### 1. Think before you act

Winners know that under pressure they always have more time than they feel they have. Taking the time for T-CUP is never a waste of time – it always saves time. Get into the habit of taking a pause for positive thought.

### 2. Stay focused

Always keep the ultimate goal in mind – winning. Don't allow yourself to be distracted. When you lose focus just remind yourself that you have achieved many times before and can do so now. A physical reminder such as a to-do list next to your computer screen, an alarm on your watch or a photograph on your fridge can help to keep you focused.

### 3. Prepare thoroughly

Do not mistake wishful thinking for positive thinking. The mistake many people make is to study the biggest achievers, hear how supremely confident they are about their chances of winning and confuse cause and effect. Winners don't win just because they parrot a few positive phrases. It's a combination of real self-belief and diligence and sticking to the winning way. Winners succeed because they have done everything they can to prepare for success. They work, think and practise like winners. That is why winners maximise their potential.

### 4. Defeat the fear of failure

Burst the tyre on the vicious circle of negativity – it's just in your head. The way to do this, especially if our self-belief is not as high as it should be, is to keep the task as simple as possible. Don't allow people to undermine you or put you off. Don't allow your mind to run away with the worst-case scenario. Block out any negative thoughts that enter your head. Almost like a parachute jumper standing in the doorway of a plane at 12,000 feet, you have to force yourself to overcome the fear, believing that you will land safely. Keep your mind on the successful end result, visualise it, and go for it. Continually remind yourself of your capabilities and your previous achievements.

## 5. Look at it differently

Can't see the wood for the trees? Making mountains out of molehills? Sometimes we are too close to the problem to see it objectively. Get a new perspective. Look at it from another person's point of view. Talk to other people about it. Force yourself to think differently – almost like playing chess against yourself. Is there anything positive you can focus on? Suddenly the problem won't seem as bad, and you might well find a solution you hadn't thought of.

## 6. Debrief continuously

Make a habit of debriefing. Give yourself credit for the successes as you go along, and evaluate how you can improve to make it less stressful next time. This will make you more efficient as you won't repeat annoying mistakes and will therefore be more positive. The problem is that when we feel down, we often don't debrief in the right way. We concentrate on, and wallow in, what went wrong. And when something goes right, we don't debrief and analyse what went right. We don't enjoy the success or figure out what we need to learn in order to repeat that success, and this dictates our state of mind. It's important to debrief positively during and after each situation to learn the lessons, fix what needs to be fixed and then move on.

## 7. Stay positive

If you have a positive self-image and self-worth, you will find ways of improving and hence enjoying your life – by constantly debriefing. This means you will continually strive to improve and focus on the positive, and that will change your state of mind. All of a sudden you will be used to, and comfortable with, success. So you won't feel like such an interloper in the winner's enclosure – it won't be an accident.

## 8. Spoil yourself

Sometimes all it takes is some pampering to make us feel better: a new haircut, a bit of retail therapy or a darn good workout in the gym. Maybe go and see someone who makes you feel good about yourself. Take some respite and have a good time and you'll feel stronger and more prepared to take on the world.

## 9. Don't be sarcastic

Resist sarcasm and cynicism. They might seem harmless enough, but they can be deceptively corrosive and indicative of a negative mindset that will eventually wear you down.

## 10. Psyche yourself up

Give yourself a running start by pumping yourself up – for example, by using the 'see no evil, hear no evil, speak no evil' tactics from the last chapter (see page 46). Get the adrenaline flowing and you won't know your own mental strength.

# FOUR

# HOW TO PUT WINNING METHODS INTO PRACTICE

## GOALS

- ☑ to learn the value of planning the winning way and how to do it
- ☑ to put the winning mindset into practice
- ☑ to build on successes as well as celebrate them
- ☑ to learn positively from setbacks instead of dwelling negatively on them
- ☑ to maintain the momentum of success so that it becomes a lifestyle, not a one-off

## THE SECRET OF SUCCESS

If you truly want to figure out how and why something apparently complicated works, it's often a good idea to dismantle it and see how the constituent parts operate and fit together (although this doesn't work for toasters). In the same way, if you want to know how and why something is successful, you can reduce it to simpler, bite-size chunks. The purpose of this chapter is to do precisely that, because once you know how and why success happens, you can begin to make your own replica successes.

# THE WINNING BEHAVIOUR CYCLE

In all my years of studying and analysing successful people, I have gradually identified and refined what it is that makes them successful by breaking down their achievements. So what is their secret to success? Their secret is that there really is no secret: their successes are based on a regular pattern of behaviour. It is what I call the 'winning behaviour cycle'. The good news is that it's exactly what you already do yourself when you succeed and accomplish your goals. Winning is simply a case of making yourself aware and conscious of these actions so that you can deliberately replicate them in future. Once you know what this regular pattern of behaviour is, it's easy for anyone to copy.

You should now be familiar with the winning model (warrior–thinker–skill refiner–continuous debriefer). Into that model fit the winning behaviours of T-CUP (Thinking Correctly Under Pressure). The first three winning behaviours of T-CUP form the winning behaviour cycle. This is the cycle that winners go through in order to maximise their opportunity for success and minimise the possibility of failure. These three stages, which I shall then go on to explain in more detail, are as follows:

1. **Creating the opportunity**
   Preparation: opening the window of opportunity.
2. **Seizing the opportunity**
   Action: going through the window of opportunity and transforming the opportunity into real accomplishments.

## 3. Maintaining the momentum

Continuation: in terms of:

a. securing success – not taking our eye off the ball

b. perpetuating the success so that it becomes a lifestyle, not a fluke

c. maintaining your highest standards and not allowing any setbacks to slow the momentum.

## 1. CREATING THE OPPORTUNITY

We know that preparation is key if we want to succeed. The Scouts' motto is 'Be prepared', and we've all heard the old maxim, 'Fail to prepare and prepare to fail.' But in today's hectic, time-poor world, so many of us would prefer to just get on with it. We don't want to spend ages looking at the map, as we know roughly where the wedding is taking place. We don't want to pore over a manual full of instructions; we'd prefer just to work out how the camera operates by pressing a few buttons. We don't want to read a book telling us how to be a winner; we just want it to happen straight away. The trouble is, skipping the preparation stage often wastes far more time in the long run, and causes us much more unnecessary stress and disappointment. We might miss the turning on the motorway and arrive at the wedding all hot and bothered halfway through the first hymn. If we don't study the instruction booklet, we might fail to capture on camera that precious moment when our son scores his first goal. And if you skim-read this book and miss out all the practical exercises, you won't learn nearly as much about winning as you should!

The bottom line is that a lack of preparation sees us end up losing much more than we gain.

For a winner, the success of every single thing we do in life depends on preparation to a greater or lesser degree, whether it's as trivial as remembering to buy some milk or as important as figuring out a way to win a huge new contract at work. A winner does not rely on luck or chance, for by their very nature these things are unreliable. Winners make their own luck by not leaving anything to chance. That's why you might look at a very successful person and say, 'But they are so lucky…' In actual fact, they are probably just better prepared. Herein lies that difference between wishing and positive thinking again: positive thinkers don't just hope for the best; they do everything in their power to ensure it.

It's important to focus not just on the ultimate goal of success, but also on the process of getting there. This doesn't mean you have to draw up a grand master plan every time you want to buy some groceries, but if you don't write a shopping list, for example, then you're likely to forget a few key items. Of course, with life's more important tasks, we do tend to formulate some kind of plan. But how effective is it? Could it be improved? Does everything always go according to our plan? If not, do we have a contingency?

By preparing the ground the winner's way, you create an opportunity to succeed. The more appropriate that preparation (and appropriate is not always synonymous with thoroughness if time is precious), the wider that window of opportunity and thus the greater your chance of success.

## TO DO: Success in 60 seconds

Think of a particular task you have got to do this week. It might be picking up your parents from the airport, completing your tax return or hitting a big deadline at work. Jot it down below. Underneath, write down exactly what you would consider to be a success when it comes to performing that task. Spend no more than 20 seconds doing this. Leave 'the plan' blank for now.

*The task:*
*Desired success:*
*The plan:*

Your desired success might be as simple as completing the task. Fine. Or it might be that you'd like to have that difficult conversation with your parents on the way home, or perhaps you'd like to learn how you could reduce your tax bill, or maybe you'd like to train up a junior to take on the project next time...

The truth is you will benefit by having your success defined in terms of clear, specific and tangible results. Only when you have a very clear idea of what you're aiming for in terms of measurable results can you get to the next stage: making a list of the preconditions necessary to achieve that goal. The following table illustrates what is meant by measurable, as opposed to non-measurable, results.

| GENERIC – NON-MEASURABLE RESULTS | SPECIFIC – MEASURABLE RESULTS |
|---|---|
| I'd like to cut down on smoking | I'm going to give up completely |
| I'd like to be better at computing | I'm going to learn to touch-type |
| We're going to increase productivity | We're aiming to increase productivity by 30 per cent over the next six months |

Now go back to your task and write down 'the plan' as a list of things you need to do in order to achieve your desired success. For example, if it's the tax form you need to fill in, the preconditions might include getting all your pay slips together, downloading helpful hints from the Internet, speaking to your friend who is an accountant, giving yourself a deadline by which to get the form finished, and so on. Spend no more than 30 seconds doing this.

Done? There, in 60 seconds you have set yourself a well-defined target and devised a plan for hitting it. See how simple this is, even if you don't necessarily write it down? If you're prepared to invest just a minute or so of your time to 'create the opportunity for your desired success', you can greatly increase the chances of achieving it. Pausing to think for a minute like this could save you hours in the long run, and a lot of stress.

Once this list of preconditions has been written down or carefully thought through, a winner would go through it and tick them off one by one until each has been satisfied. Any that cannot be ticked off must be dealt with. This is a way to highlight the gaps between failure and success, and it helps to keep you focused on your specific target(s).

## More speed, less haste

If a minute's planning can make such a big difference, why don't more people do it? Because it takes a lot of willpower to fight old habits, that's why, but that is all part of the warrior–thinker–skill refiner–continuous debriefer's winning mindset. If you're hasty, be a warrior and a thinker and make the change to winning behaviour: create the opportunity properly; strive for the best possible result through refining your skills; avoid unnecessary corners through preplanning and debriefing. The desire to succeed should outweigh the desire to blunder in without pausing for thought.

(Of course, sometimes pausing to plan is inappropriate if time is short, such as when we are pressed to make a snap decision. However, having prepared for such a situation, a winner will have thought beforehand about what is best to do. A supposedly snap decision is therefore informed by snap thinking: 'I know what I have to do in this situation.' It's the mental equivalent of *Blue Peter*: 'Here's a thought I had earlier.' You can train your instincts and your intuition. That's why you practise emergency stops when you learn to drive, comedians learn instant put-downs for hecklers, and politicians develop stalling/evasion tactics when asked tricky questions on the spot.)

## More speed, less waste

The same is true for the person who constantly strives for perfection. Although this sounds laudable, in reality it's sometimes not very helpful and can often lead to a wasted opportunity. Is anything ever perfect? How do you know when it is good enough? While we're waiting for or trying to create the perfect conditions, the opportunity may just pass us by. Like the surfer waiting in the water for the perfect wave, you need to spot the opportunity coming, get ready and then go for it. Otherwise it all might just wash over you.

The secret is in the timing. The window of opportunity will not stay open forever. By continuously debriefing and learning from past experience, a winner learns to know when to go for it. A winner does seek perfection, but not at the expense of taking the opportunity. So winners are practical perfectionists: they go for the best possible result. 'Perfect' and 'best possible' are not necessarily synonymous. So if, for example, having a business report professionally printed and bound would mean potentially missing the deadline, a winner would avoid that unnecessary corner by foreseeing it and making a judgement call to print the documents in-house. The quality may not be quite as good, but at least the whole success of the project has not been jeopardised. Winning is about making the best of any situation.

## How to maximise the opportunity for success

### Plan

Create the opportunity for your desired success. A winner won't just dive in without thinking first, even if it's just a second or two's preparation. This is because winners do not take unnecessary risks and chances. They stick to tried-and-tested methods that work. Get in the habit of sitting down at the start of each day and before each task, and think through what your desired success is. You'll find your efficiency improves a great deal.

### Debrief

It is impossible to overstate the importance of debriefing in the context of winning. I refer to it constantly and make no apology for doing so. Continuous debriefing helps us stay on the right path – a route on which there is rarely any congestion – through a process of real-time self-checking. It's like a word-processing program that automatically backs itself up, or a sea swimmer who pops his head well above the surface every few strokes to make sure he is heading in the right direction. It therefore builds up our self-awareness and means that we never go too far wrong. It also makes the process of winning much quicker and more efficient. Through reviewing our actions – both in real-time and in retrospect – we learn what works and what does not so that we can repeat the successes and edit out any failures.

You need to become so familiar with the process of continuously debriefing that it imbeds itself in your intuition like a reflex. This will come with practise and repetition until it is so automatic you barely even have to think about it. It's as simple as taking a brief moment every now and then to look at:

▶ what your ultimate desired success is
▶ what you're doing at that precise time
▶ making sure the two are aligned.

If not, then you need to adjust or reset your actions until they are. This means that you don't waste time, energy and resources carrying on regardless down a path that will ultimately lead to failure. Remember: making mistakes is normal, but winners don't repeat them. Checking your progress and learning from experience means you will make the most of any opportunity.

**Back-up**
Winners have a plan B and C as well as a plan A, but these plans will also be tried and tested. It is not a case of experimenting in a crucial situation; rather, it's a case of implementing the right plan for the circumstances. Back-up plans are another insurance measure to guard against failure. It's rather like how a sports team might practise set-plays so that when it comes to the match situation, they are ready and prepared with a game-plan and a set of rehearsed moves that can be implemented where appropriate.

**Simulate**
Visualising the expected scenarios in our minds makes us more prepared, and less likely to face something we hadn't considered. Many people find role-playing various possibilities to be helpful in terms of preparation. This could take the form of thinking up the kinds of question you expect to be asked in an exam, an interview or at the end of a presentation so that nothing takes you unawares. It might also be helpful to imagine how you would react if anything goes wrong, so that you are well-prepared in any case.

Concentrating on the process of achieving our desired success, as opposed to just thinking about the success itself, tends to make us more focused and purposeful.

**Practise**

Winners want to win. So they put every effort into making sure that happens: by preparing, by minimising risk and by practising. This is the skill-refining stage of the winning behaviour model. As part of creating the opportunity for their desired success, winners practise and perfect so much that it ends up looking like a pure gift or talent when it is in fact the result of a heck of a lot of work. This is why some people are great at giving presentations, others are superb at tennis and a few are brilliant at reverse parallel parking. Not many people naturally enjoy putting in lots of effort, and winners are the same, but the difference is that they fight their natural tendencies to stop or give up. This self-discipline to go through the pain barrier comes from the warrior part of the winning behaviour model. But it's a lot easier to find the motivation when it brings success.

## 2. SEIZING THE OPPORTUNITY

Action time. This is the second stage of the winning behaviour cycle. For impatient people, this is often step one, while perfectionists and procrastinators may not even get to this stage. Again, a key factor here is timing. You can't be impetuous and jump in too soon, but nor can you delay forever and miss the opportunity altogether. You need to be a practical perfectionist.

Moving from the 'dreaming' of stage one to the 'doing' of stage two is the moment of truth when some people freeze or fail to deliver. We can all talk a good game, but delivering is another matter. We need a winning mindset to make the most of any opportunity. This will enable us to overcome two types of blocks to success:

1. Inner obstacles – subjective limitations: over-confidence, complacency, fears (of failure, of success), lack of confidence/self-belief, perceived lack of experience and/or skills, physical and mental fatigue. It's the devil on our shoulder.

2. External obstacles – objective limitations: the opponent, the target/goal, level of difficulty, the environment (finances, facilities, experience, and so on.)

To seize the opportunity and make the most of it, you need to employ the following T-CUP principles we outlined in Chapter 1.

## Stick to what works and leave behind what doesn't

You've come up with a plan. You know what your desired success is and what you have to do to get it. So stick to the game-plan as long as it delivers results. Your instincts might tell you to improvise, to take short cuts or try something different – 'It only took me 20 minutes to get there last time; I bet I can get it down to 15' – but when in crucial situations, resist this temptation. By continually debriefing, winners are able to stick to what works and jettison what doesn't: 'It took me 20 minutes last time. That means I need to allow 25 minutes this time in case there are any delays.'

## Get back to basics

What are the 'basics' – the essential foundations – in your life? Do you know? This is a question I ask all the people I work with, and the vast majority don't know. And therein lies half their problem, basically.

If you lose concentration or stray from the plan, you need to get back to recognisable landmarks. This is your default position – a point of strength and stability. Rather than making it up as you go along and hoping that you work it out in the end, get back to what you know and go from there.

I can remember asking the manager of a world-famous football team what his basics were, and he didn't know either. He'd never thought about things this way. We talked about it and eventually decided that the basics, as far as his team was concerned, were all the set-plays in terms of both defending and attacking: free kicks, corners, throw-ins, penalties. 'Right,' I said. 'First things first. Let's set about practising and refining those. Then everything else will follow.' These are the nuts and bolts of football. It meant that every time the game stopped, his team could seize control of the situation from the restart. They could practise those basics in training and measure their success from the match statistics.

Winning is about reducing your life to its manageable, measurable chunks and controlling them – a little like a recipe. It's decoding an art and converting it into a science. The more you can control, the less chance there is of things going wrong, and so the more you can dictate success. The basics are your safety net, your building blocks on which the rest of your success is founded. But for most of us, the basics are so basic we almost don't even think about them. They are second nature. But unless we are aware of them, we cannot effectively control them.

How do you know what your basics are? This is something you need to draw up for yourself. Think through the following examples.

▶ If you're a manager, you need to make sure that your staff are productive, profitable and happy, and that you are meeting your targets. If you allow yourself to be preoccupied by board level problems or distracted by what the opposition are doing, you could find that your neglected team starts to fall apart. The team you manage is 'your basics'. Get that right and keep it right before you worry about anything else.

▶ If you're a restaurateur then the basics are producing good-quality food and service so that people will come back again and spread the word. But if you're more concerned with opening a new restaurant or maximising profits in the short term, then you may find the basics suffer, leaving you with no customers to go to your new restaurant and no profits in the long term.

▶ If you're a parent then your basics are to provide security, a home, food, clothing, love, support and opportunities for your children, and to set them the best possible example you can.

▶ If you are a salesperson, what are your basics? Maybe it's having good-quality product examples and an effective and knowledgeable sales pitch. These basics are easily measurable – by how many you sell.

▶ If you're a teacher, what are your basics? It might be having thorough and appropriate lesson plans, having enough materials for the class, and seeing progress from your pupils...

Again, all these areas are measurable, so if you're not mastering your basics you can soon see where you need to improve. For every basic you identify there is another level – your operational basic. This will show you *how* to improve and give you the tools to find a solution. So once you have found solutions to your common problems, these solutions form part of your basics. Winning is not trial and error, but trial and refinement.

---

### THINK: What are your basics?

Rather like having a job description or a foolproof recipe to follow, it can be helpful to see these things written down as a point of future reference in order to increase your awareness of them.

1. It's often easier to look at someone else's basics to help you define your own. What would you say the basics for success are for the following: a surgeon, a gardener, a shopkeeper, a police officer...?

2. Now think about the basics of your own job. Try and come up with at least five fundamentals.

3. Figure out what your basics are for the most important areas of your life – the critical areas in which you cannot afford to fail. You can also do this for the other areas of your life on your 'problem pages' (see Chapter 1).

---

4. Think about ways in which these areas can be measured or controlled so that you can evaluate your performance by looking at the statistics (for instance, sales, pupils' grades, successful operations performed). Give yourself a percentage mark for how well you think you are performing those basics right now.

5. Write a note in your diary to reassess these marks in one month's time to evaluate your progress. Just by reminding yourself of your basics on a regular basis, your performance will improve.

## 3. MAINTAINING THE MOMENTUM

Stage three works alongside stages one and two, completing and perpetuating the cycle. It's the part that helps the winner to maximise success, minimise failure and continue to improve so that winning is not a sporadic or temporary experience but a continuous and ongoing lifestyle. Maintaining the momentum after a success reflects the strength of the winner's warrior mindset.

### The danger of complacency

Winning often gives you a great confidence boost. The danger is that it can make you complacent – and that is when you are most vulnerable to messing it all up. It's like the fable of the tortoise and the hare. The hare thought he was so sure of beating the tortoise in a race that he could win in his sleep. Of course, his complacency was his undoing, and the slow but steady tortoise won through. Winners don't take their foot off the pedal like this. Their attitude is not to take anything for granted, for to do so implies taking an unnecessary risk.

Maintaining the momentum is also about safeguarding success. For example, you might have won some great business for your company, but if you subsequently become too complacent and neglect your clients, you could lose them and your good reputation to boot. Fight back: be creative, improve your product, be number one in service. Similarly, you might have lost a lot of weight, but if you immediately go back to your old ways after achieving that success, you will regain your old weight. If you maintain healthy eating and exercise habits, you'll be able to keep your success going. Continue to behave in the way you did until the point at which you achieved success. Keep your standards up.

---

## When practice makes perfect

Clive Woodward once showed me a quote from an old book called *Theory of Modern Rugby* written in 1930 by I.M.B Stuart, an assistant master at Harrow School. It refers to rugby, but the general attitude is one that could explain why the British winning mindset is underdeveloped.

*We have taught the world games, we have taught the world the true spirit in which to play those games, and if we no longer hold pride of place as players of the game, it matters nothing so long as we British always continue to be looked up to as the truest 'players of the game' in the world. That is our greatest heritage and one that I trust will be regarded as our most closely guarded possession – that the prize counts for nothing in comparison with the spirit in which it is struggled for. In other words, that the spirit of the game is the prize.*

*We wonder why it is that other countries can defeat us at most sports, and the answer is to be found not in that they are physically more endowed than we are, but that they have the temperament to practise doggedly their weakness, and endeavour to improve before they proceed any further. The Englishman, on the other hand, refuses to identify his weakness and*

---

*practise assiduously to correct it. For this reason the average Rugby footballer cannot place-kick. He refuses to practise what he calls 'drudge work', except just now and then.*

It was this mentality and attitude that Clive and I were battling when working with the England rugby coaches. How fitting it was that it was the boot of Jonny Wilkinson that kicked England to victory. That winning drop kick was the centre point of a strategy that England had practised over and over again; Wilkinson performed the assigned task that he'd practised thousands of hours to accomplish. His story is the exact opposite of the spirit that has seemed to form the prevailing culture of English sport for centuries.

## Build on success

It can be difficult to maintain the momentum like this when all you really want to do is to enjoy your success, but there is a very good reason for doing so. It is something I work on with many of my clients, especially where business and sports teams are involved. Debriefing during and after a success is crucial for maintaining momentum because then you can spot what went right, isolate those factors and make sure you repeat them. Most people debrief and conduct inquiries only after failures. Although it is useful to learn from your mistakes, dwelling on the negative can be destructive because it can foster a negative mindset. Instead, dwell on the positive and draw from it. It's easier for success to breed success if the breeding conditions are optimal. So why not create them?

This is where most people have it all wrong. I believe that all too often in all spheres of life, but especially business and sport, people make too much of defeat and too little of success. They should be treated with equal care and importance. When you lose a big business deal, you're normally hauled into the boardroom for an inquiry to find out what went wrong. When you win a big deal, on the other hand, you're normally taken straight down to the pub to celebrate. It should be the other way around. When you win the big deal, that's when you should analyse what went right and how you can learn from your success to do it again the next time. However, when things go wrong, sometimes the last thing you want to do is dwell on the mistakes. It's fine to do something else to distract yourself from being eaten away by it, but remember to debrief your mistake at some point otherwise you won't learn from it.

When you have a setback, it's important to realise it is only that – it's not the end of the world. People see failure as 'a sign that it just wasn't meant to be'. Rubbish! Be a warrior and fight these thoughts. Winners know that long-term success is never linear; it's up and down, but the overall pattern is an upward learning curve. Be tough, and increase your pain threshold where difficulty and effort are concerned because this is the real world. You don't become a winner after one single success and you don't become a loser after a single failure. Such knee-jerk reactions (whether they be on the sports pages or in the minutes of the board meeting) are unhelpful. Being a winner means that you experience a relatively high frequency of success. Winners enjoy far more ups than downs because they learn from the ups and they learn from the downs. That's how the frequency of winning increases. And in order to experience that, you just have to behave according to the winning behaviour cycle.

To be a winner you have to learn how to build on successes when you experience them and how to minimise the damage to your self-confidence and self-belief when you experience disappointments. You can limit the effect of a setback by:

▶ choosing to think positively about it in accordance with the winning mindset

▶ resolving to learn from it through effective debriefing

▶ using it as motivation to improve, refusing to be beaten by it or to give up, even when the going gets tough.

If you do all that, you will not lose too much of the momentum you've built up. If I promised you that you'd never experience failure again, I'd be a liar. That's life – but it's about how you respond to a failure that matters. In order to win, you have to know how to lose; you have to know how to handle your setbacks in order to move forwards.

## TO DO: Family fortunes of success

As an essential exercise in debriefing, breaking events down to their constituent parts helps you raise your awareness of the ingredients of both success and failure.

A. SUCCESS

▶ Think back to a success you recently experienced. It could be hitting a sales target, passing a driving test or an exam, getting a new job or promotion, going on a great holiday or buying a house.

▶ Discounting luck, try and think of the reasons why you succeeded. Come up with five reasons and rank them in order of importance. Keep thinking until you've got five good ones.

▶ Next, try and categorise the reasons you give so that you can see where your strengths lie, where you went right and what lesson(s) you can learn for future reference so that you can repeat the success. An example of how this might look is set out below.

**SUCCESS:** Getting a new job

| RANK | REASON | CATEGORY |
|------|--------|----------|
| 1. | I prepared answers to likely interview questions really well | Preparation |
| 2. | I took my time in the interview and didn't get flustered | Performance |
| 3. | I researched the company thoroughly | Preparation |
| 4. | My CV and application were both strong | Preparation |
| 5. | I wore a new suit that made me feel really smart | Confidence |

**Debrief**

**Result:** I got the job mainly because of my thorough preparation. That also helped boost my confidence and calm my nerves in the interview. I stuck to my game-plan and did not change tactics when I felt that it was working.

**Lesson to learn:** In future, I will make sure that I spend similar time and effort preparing so that I can maximise my performance. I will repeat the part of my strategy that worked so well for me.

B. SETBACK

Now go through the same process for a failure you recently experienced. It might be something as basic as missing a train, forgetting a friend's birthday or perhaps pulling a muscle during a tennis match. It might be something far more serious such as a relationship that broke down, or losing a big client at work. Discounting bad luck, think of the top five reasons for the setback and categorise them so that you can identify where you went wrong. This should give you a good pointer as to where you can improve in future so that mistakes are not repeated.

**SETBACK:** Missed deadline at work

| RANK | REASON | CATEGORY |
|------|--------|----------|
| 1. | I always miss deadlines | Bad habit |
| 2. | I had too many other things on my plate | Overwork |
| 3. | The subject matter bored me | Lack of enthusiasm |
| 4. | I didn't plan the task properly | Poor preparation |
| 5. | I should have delegated some of the task | Poor preparation |

**Debrief**

**Result:** I missed the deadline because I was not motivated or organised enough to hit it.

**Lessons to learn:** I need to look at working back from the deadline to organise my time and workload more effectively. I also need to get a more positive mindset.

# PUT THE CHAMPAGNE ON ICE

We can learn from repetition. Next time you have a big success, just take a moment before you get swept away in the celebrations to debrief: consider why you achieved and how you can repeat that success. Then go and celebrate a job well done.

Next time you experience a setback, leave the post-mortem till the next day. Just for once, try not to dwell on it and develop a negative mindset. Go and do something else. Take your mind off it. Take your team or your partner out for a meal; go for a long walk; watch a film; sleep on it. Then the next day, before you forget, debrief and have a look at what positives you can draw from the experience and what mistakes should not be repeated. Don't let the process of debriefing allow you to always lay the blame on external factors. It is important to also look at yourself for where things went wrong.

# FIVE

# HOW TO CREATE YOUR OWN LUCK

## GOALS

☑ to learn how best to react to unavoidable problems
☑ to realise how to avoid unnecessary corners
☑ to know when to trust your intuition
☑ to understand how to simplify life
☑ to create winners' 'luck'

## THE STRESS TEST

Three friends of similar intelligence are doing some last-minute revision before a big professional exam.

Jill sits and stares at her books and realises how much she still doesn't know. The more she thinks, the more upset and distressed she gets. What if the subjects she has focused her revision on don't come up in the exam? Why didn't she start her revision earlier? Why can't she be lucky like Sarah who always gets grade As without even seeming to try? Jill resolves to stay up all night cramming until her highlighter pens have run out of ink and she has run out of energy. She sleeps badly and wakes up the next morning exhausted, having hardly taken in a thing she passively 'read' last night. She race-reads more notes until the last possible moment before rushing into the exam hall a bundle of nerves, convinced she is going to fail and swearing she will never take another exam.

Adam is also looking at his books and he too realises just how much he still doesn't know. However, it's the night before the exam: the last thing he needs to do is cram his head full of half-understood material that will only confuse him and stress him out. He knows he's quite clever and somehow managed to fluke a good pass last time so he'll probably get through this one the same. He resolves to chill out and take his mind off the exam by watching a film until he dozes off to sleep. He wakes feeling calm and relaxed and saunters into the exam hall, winking at Jill who is scrabbling around on the floor for some reason as he takes his seat.

Sarah has also been quite stressed about how much material there was to learn, but she has stuck to a strict and well-planned studying timetable. Rather than spend the night before the exam learning new material, she decides to consolidate what she already knows by practising essay plans using past exam papers. She gets an early night, reading a good novel to help her get to sleep. She wakes early and is nervous, but knows she has prepared as well as she could have done and she thrives on this kind of adrenaline. She arrives at the exam hall in good time and goes through her practised exam technique in her head – read the questions thoroughly, spend 30 minutes per question, and so on – and doesn't notice Adam making faces at her, or Jill dropping her pens all over the floor.

The same situation but three different ways of dealing with it. Which one acted like a winner? The answer is easy – Sarah. Why did she succeed where the others did not?

It's not because she is cleverer than either of them – their IQs are roughly the same.

It's not because she is very lucky, as Jill jealously thinks.

Sarah has made her own 'luck' because she has employed the winning behaviours of T-CUP to simplify the task and fulfil her winning potential. Let's check back through them to see exactly how she has done this.

1. **Create the opportunity** – Through thorough exam preparation and revision.
2. **Seize the opportunity** – By getting into the right frame of mind and practising effective exam techniques to perform on the day.
3. **Maintain the momentum** – She was committed to the highest possible standards and was able to use her past experience of getting A-grades to attain another top mark.
4. **Strive for the best possible result** – She practised thoroughly and remained committed to her timetable and overall plan.
5. **Avoid unnecessary corners** – She didn't allow herself to be distracted by more enjoyable activities during the revision stage. She didn't waste time the night before or get herself all worked up. She didn't rest on past successes like Adam, or expect to do badly like Jill.
6. **Stick to what works** – Through debriefing, she repeated the same steps that got her an A-grade in the past.
7. **Give up what doesn't work** – And she weeded out the techniques that didn't work so well previously.
8. **Get back to basics** – Preparation, exam technique, time management, rest.

9. **Improve your self-control** – She had the discipline to put in the work, and through exercising self-control she was able to control her nerves and combat negative thinking.

10. **Make the correct decisions** – From choosing what to revise and when (perhaps making sacrifices such as staying in to work) to answering the right questions on the day, Sarah's decision-making was excellent, as was her transition to the actual execution of the plan.

11. **Learn to thrive under pressure** – She wasn't too flustered like Jill or too relaxed like Adam. She simplified her task. By preparing well, managing her time and exercising self-control, Sarah learned how to cope. Reminding herself of how well she performed on past exam papers had a huge contribution to strengthening her self-belief.

12. **Maximise your use of time** – From drawing up her prioritised revision timetable to finding time to stick to it, to going through her last-minute routine (including resting), to performing in the exam hall... Sarah displayed excellent time management and remembered that under pressure you have more time than you feel you have.

We all know people like these three. When faced with a problem or a hard task, we might even be able to see ourselves in one of them. But the fact is Jill and Adam could also be winners. The reason they did not succeed in this case is principally because they did not simplify the task. This chapter is going to explain how you can do precisely that so that you can increase your chances of success. Winners make their own luck by not leaving anything to chance.

# Do you feel lucky?

Many people rely on luck. Some believe in lucky heather, while others are very superstitious and won't walk under ladders or arrange anything on Friday 13th. Others still would prefer to call it fate or destiny, or maybe even Providence. While life undoubtedly has elements of chance – and that is part of what makes life interesting – it makes no rational sense to conduct one's life according to luck. Because luck by its very nature is not rational. Every so often we will experience good luck and bad luck. But it makes no sense to rely on good luck to succeed and to blame bad luck if we fail.

Research has shown that people who think of themselves as unlucky are also more likely to be superstitious. Why? Because unlucky people tend to rely on ineffective – perhaps even irrational – ways of dealing with difficult situations they face. Avoiding the cracks in the pavement on the way to the exam would not have helped Sarah get her A-grade. Being a warrior, a thinker, a skill refiner and a debriefer had far more influence. It enabled her to stick to a plan that had worked in the past and to avoid unnecessary corners (what other people might attribute to 'bad luck'). This brings truth to the old maxim that in life we make our own luck. Just as professional gamblers make a living by reducing elements of chance, so winners do likewise with life. And that way they can 'beat the system'. Often success may appear to others on the outside as being 'lucky' – and every so often, it is. But if a lot of hard and effective work has gone into that success, it is not lucky; it's winning behaviour. Attributing success to luck means that we might not learn from our success so that we can replicate it.

By the same token, disappointments and failure are often seen to be the result of bad luck. But if no adequate plan was put in place to ensure success (that is, poor creation of the opportunity), then it's not really bad luck; it's bad preparation. If you go to a business meeting without doing your research or knowing your facts and figures, is the subsequent loss of that client down to bad luck? No, you failed to prepare the opportunity properly for your desired success. If you're rushing around and forget to lock your car properly and it is stolen, is that purely bad luck? No, you didn't take enough care so you put yourself in an unnecessary corner. If you put every effort into doing the best that you can – into following the winning behaviours of T-CUP – you will be more in control of the variables. Blaming bad luck is not debriefing the winning way. It means that we do not take responsibility for the failure and thus will not learn from it to improve next time.

## HOW WINNERS AVOID UNNECESSARY CORNERS

One of the most surprising discoveries I have made in my research of winners is that, behind the scenes, the vast majority of them are not at all what other people imagine they are. Far from being superheroes with a magic touch, they are actually very pragmatic, hard-working people. They develop their skills through courageous and continuous debriefing so that they are constantly improving. But they are also able to make the most of those skills and maximise their full potential because they know how to simplify every task they face. How?

▶ They don't leave things to the last minute.
▶ They don't try and get by without doing any preparation.
▶ They don't experiment in crucial situations.
▶ They start with their practised game-plan rather than improvising.
▶ They just keep things very simple.

The truth is, very few of us make life simple. We tend to overcomplicate it by trying to take short cuts, being complacent or ill-disciplined, or being too smart, thinking we know it all. When we are able to disentangle or simplify a task, it obviously becomes easier to complete.

## DEBRIEF YOURSELF

At the end of the last chapter, I asked you to focus on a situation that had gone wrong for you. Cast your mind back to it again. Would you agree that the situation became more complicated than it needed to be? Perhaps you should have allowed for bad traffic and left for the station a little earlier to ensure you didn't miss your train. Perhaps you should write all your friends' birthdays in your diary, as you have been meaning to do for ages, so you don't forget them. Maybe you should have arrived for the match a bit earlier so you could have warmed up properly and not pulled a muscle. When things go wrong, we often blame ourselves retrospectively for messing it up:

▶ not being on the ball enough
▶ wasting time
▶ not leaving ourselves enough time
▶ not preparing adequately
▶ repeating wrong techniques.

But if we had learned from our mistakes the last time, we wouldn't keep making them. It is through debriefing and raising our self-awareness that we learn from our mistakes. But how many of us debrief effectively after a success and take note of what, why and how we did well so that we can replicate those techniques? That commitment is the key.

The more important or critical a situation, the more likely we are to make an effort to ensure it goes well. That's when we employ 'one-step-ahead thinking', to see those 'corners' coming up. In being aware and thinking ahead, we are naturally more prepared for any potential obstacles or problems, and are therefore more likely to be able to avoid them altogether. For example, in the case of the missed train, we might think ahead and realise that the traffic outside the station will probably be busy at 5.30pm and that the ticket queues are longer in rush hour. So we might resolve to buy our ticket online first and leave home 15 minutes earlier so that we are not stressed and panicking about time. If we get there early, we might have time to get a newspaper and find a good seat.

In other words, from time to time we all use the winner's technique of avoiding unnecessary corners, even though we might not realise it – it just comes naturally. But in order to increase the frequency of success (regardless of its level of importance) we need to increase the frequency of *deliberately* avoiding such obstacles whenever possible – not just in crucial situations. We are talking here about forming a winning habit, adapting to a winning way of life. This has the triple benefit of:

1. ensuring we won't encounter failure so often
2. shortening and streamlining our route to success in future
3. significantly strengthening our self-belief and perception of self-worth.

You see how simple it is? No grand strategy or complicated tactics. No need for amazing natural talent or intellect. No need to rely on luck or chance. Just do the same things you do when the situation is critical and you won't slip up half as often. Avoiding unnecessary corners should come as standard, like airbags in a new car. Then you'd be well on your way to achieving more success more often. This is precisely what winners do.

So if it really is this simple, why don't we already do it? Because there is one key difference between winners and everyone else: an intolerance of failure. Winners do not accept it and will take proactive steps to avoid it, no matter the scale of the challenge. For winners, success is the be-all and end-all. Failure does not enter into the equation. Therefore all corners must be consistently avoided as a matter of course. This is how winning becomes a habit and self-belief becomes strengthened.

---

## How to avoid unnecessary corners

In order to avoid unnecessary corners, we need to be able to identify, by mapping, what those corners are in the first place. As a definition, 'corners' are anything that might lead us to make an unnecessary, costly mistake. Look at potential corners in your working life, social relationships and so on. By labelling a given action as a corner, there is a good chance that you won't get stuck there any more.

---

In important, crucial situations, most of us will try our best and put some effort in. If we haven't learned from past experience, it might not be the most effective effort, but at least we are trying. However, when the situation is less crucial, many of us tend to put in less effort and are less disciplined. It's human nature. Perhaps we will rely too much on intuition to get us through – and that can lead to over-confidence and complacency. Or we will allow other things to take priority such as five more minutes in bed when we're in danger of running late, or trying to take a risky short cut...

---

## A short conversation about the short cut to success

Some common challenges to my theory are as follows:

*'How do winners streamline the route to success?'*
The irony is that in not *taking* a short cut to success, winners *find* a short cut to success. This is because the winning way is a process of continual refinement and increased efficiency. If you cut out what doesn't work and only do what does work, you won't waste time – you will maximise it. This means that you will experience success more quickly as well as more frequently.

---

*'But surely failing every now and then is part of the fun, and makes success all the sweeter when it comes?'*
The winning way does not preclude fun; it just doesn't put it at the expense of success. Avoid getting trapped in unnecessary corners and enjoy the fun of success.

*'It all sounds a bit robotic. To err is human after all, and if we never experimented, we'd never progress.'*
Winners do experiment and use their creativity, just not in critical situations when their strategy is working fine and experimentation might jeopardise success. Winners experiment at the right time and in the right place. They do take calculated risks when it's needed, but will never take unnecessary risks. They experiment methodically in practice to come up with workable contingency plans and improvements, but when performing they stick to a tried-and-tested, proven method. The winning process is one of continual improvement.

## WHAT HAPPENS WHEN WE PUT OURSELVES UNDER UNNECESSARY PRESSURE?

Getting into unnecessary corners can often create complications that lead us to experience undue pressure. And that is when we can get upset and anxious, and even start to panic. Of course, some people thrive when put under a certain amount of pressure; others freeze or collapse; others react without thought or, therefore, control. Although some of us might need a bit of pressure to function, we all have a limit as to how much pressure we can handle. So for all of us, especially those who tend to fall apart under real pressure, it is a good policy to try and limit the amount of pressure we put ourselves under so that we can control it. This is simply because, any way you look at it, putting ourselves under undue pressure can risk or limit our chances of success and inhibit our ability to perform smoothly and effectively. Often this is because many of us tend not to think about the best approach when we are put under pressure – we just do what feels right at the time and trust our intuition. Thinking, as mentioned before, is perceived as a time consumer, and so when there is no time, there is no thought. When our intuition is good (informed by past experience and debriefing), then great. But if our intuition is bad (because of ineffective debriefing), then the problem gets a whole lot worse. Either way, winners do not rely solely on intuition for it is a difficult variable to control and thus implies risk or chance. For that reason, winners will always try and reduce unnecessary pressure.

Using the term 'unnecessary pressure' presupposes there is such a thing as necessary pressure. Stress and pressure are normally thought of as negative – with deleterious effects on our health and wellbeing. But what about those people who enjoy a certain amount of stress? This enjoyment of stress explains why some people don't settle easily into retirement, or get terribly frustrated on holiday. Pressure can be very motivating because it helps us focus and gives us an adrenaline rush. Turning pressure and stress into a positive, learning to perform under pressure and how to reduce the negative effects of pressure is something we will return to in more detail in Chapter 8 – How to Handle Pressure.

## Have you got a funny feeling about intuition?

Sometimes we get a gut feeling about something. We might not be able to explain why, but we just know. While I would caution strongly against relying solely on intuition, I do see it as a valuable skill that can be improved for use alongside more explainable decision-making.

Intuition isn't just a random hunch; it's an educated guess. It's a feeling based on a lifetime's experience. So you might not have given this particular situation much thought, but you have given similar situations so much thought in the past that you have developed an expertise. That is why an experienced doctor in the accident and emergency department may know within a second what is wrong with someone and how to treat them. Experience has taught them what signs to look for and what to do so that it becomes almost instinctive. Intuition is also the reason why an experienced football manager may know instantly whether or not a child has got what it takes to be a great player. It's also why a parent can often know what their child is feeling. They have studied their child's expressions and reactions so closely over the years that they can read them like an expert.

The way to improve your intuition is to learn effectively and proactively from experience through debriefing to build up your awareness; to learn from what goes right and also from what goes wrong. The more you train your conscious thought processes, the more accurate your unconscious thought processes will be too.

So when do you use your intuition? Winners use it when trying to weigh up the advantages of two very different decisions. It is to be used then as a supplement to T-CUP winning behaviours, not as a wild substitute for them. Trust me: I've got a good feeling about this.

## WHAT ABOUT WHEN LIFE JUST GOES WRONG?

Of course, there are times when it seems life is just inexplicably out to get us. Perhaps we experience a tragic bereavement or an accident. Perhaps we find ourselves made redundant through no fault of our own. How we react to tough situations in life dictates their magnitude and their effect. We have to be particularly strong and brave in order to turn a painful situation around through appropriate debriefing. That is not to trivialise or 'gloss over' harsh experiences, or to try and see the positive in them if that is not fitting. Sometimes debriefing in this sense is not helpful, especially immediately afterwards. But a winner will eventually bounce back from any disappointment, bringing truth to the old maxim that 'what doesn't kill you makes you stronger'.

## TO DO: Role with it

Role-playing is a very effective way of simplifying problems and avoiding corners. It's just a more developed form of preparation through visualisation: working through as many possible scenarios as you can think of, and coming up with plans for how you would deal with each one.

The simulation helps give you some valuable understanding of the situation without necessarily having to go through the experience. And it might also elicit the best way of proceeding and dealing with any potential obstacles.

Next time you are faced with a tricky situation, role-play it. For each imaginable scenario, ask yourself: 'What would I do if that happened?'

It's all about eliminating chance and increasing control so that you cannot be caught out. The more you do this, the more you build up your resistance to problems and so the more capable you become. It's an ever-strengthening process of empowerment.

## TO DO: Think yourself lucky

Combine thinking positively with avoiding unnecessary corners as follows:

▶ What's your problem?
Look at your individual targets on your 'problem pages' once again (see Chapter 1). Identify any reasons or difficulties for these problem areas. Try and be as specific as possible.

▶ Think again

Force yourself to look at the problem areas using the winner's mindset. Choose to think about them more positively. Encourage yourself to do something proactively to improve the situation.

▶ Take control

Rather than blame the reasons on other people or circumstances, look at the issues you can take responsibility for and control. Ask yourself how you can simplify the task.

▶ Predict the future

Based on your past experience, what 'corners' can you foresee? What steps can you take to avoid or overcome those corners? Make a plan to tackle them.

▶ Keep focused

Always work back from the ultimate goal and keep it in mind as you set about achieving it one step at a time, according to your tried-and-tested game-plan. Do not allow yourself to be put off or distracted. And do not improvise unnecessarily at this stage.

# STICK TO THE PLANNED ROUTE

Piece by piece we're seeing how winning maps itself out. So far, we've learned how thinking positively (Chapter 2) can improve your self-belief (Chapter 3), combining to help us put winning theory into practice (Chapter 4). In this chapter, we've looked at how the winning mindset can help us simplify and overcome problems so that they don't get blown out of proportion and so that we can streamline our route to success. That route is on the straight and narrow where there is no congestion to hold us up and no 'corners' to get us lost.

Stick to the winning way and follow the signs to destination success. It might not always feel like the shortest or easiest route, but I guarantee it's the quickest and most effective.

# SIX

# HOW TO ACHIEVE THE BEST POSSIBLE RESULTS

## GOALS

☑ to maintain winning momentum in critical situations by sticking to what works and getting rid of what doesn't

☑ to maintain winning momentum in non-critical situations by trying out new techniques and tactics to improve your methods

☑ to learn how to perfect the basics while also learning how to be more creative

☑ to strive for the best possible result, but not necessarily perfection

# THE IMPORTANCE OF STICKING TO WHAT WORKS IN CRITICAL SITUATIONS

John is a parachute jump instructor who has done thousands of faultless jumps. There is a universally accepted method of packing parachutes to ensure they will open correctly 100 per cent of the time. However, John has developed such expertise over the years that he has designed a new, simpler method of packing the parachutes that he thinks will save time and space. And because it is simpler, it will also further cut down any margin for human error. After only a couple of tests with a dummy, John is so convinced by his new method that he decides to try it out himself to prove that it works. However, when he pulls the ripcord, the parachute catches on something and doesn't open properly. After a few seconds of trying to correct it, he has to give up and deploy the emergency reserve parachute, which is slightly impeded by the first parachute. The problems mean that he is falling slightly too fast when he lands and he breaks his leg on impact.

Sandra is a negotiator, used by the police in delicate situations to do everything from bargaining with bank robbers to talking down suicide jumpers. She has an excellent record of success using her tried-and-tested methods to find a way of gaining people's trust. However, her latest big case proved to be a nightmare. She couldn't find a way to get through to an armed robber who was extremely unpleasant to her. In the end, out of frustration and disgust, she allowed her anger to get the better of her for the first time in her career. She broke the most fundamental rule of negotiation: she shouted at the robber. He responded by wounding one of his hostages.

Anil is the captain of his Sunday league football team. He's had a great season, guiding his side to the cup final. Late in the game, the referee awards Anil's team a penalty that could win them the cup. Having successfully scored three penalties earlier in the season, Anil steps up to take it. He always places the ball in the bottom left-hand corner and it normally works. In fact, he's only ever missed once in umpteen attempts, and even then he scored on the rebound. However, in the pressure of the cup final, Anil changes his mind and decides to go for power over placement. He blasts the ball as hard as he can – unfortunately, it blazes high over the crossbar. The opposition end up scoring a winner in injury time, leaving Anil and his team-mates to reflect miserably on what might have been.

Three very different crucial situations, but three similar outcomes. By changing a proven method either out of overconfidence, frustration or panic, the success of the task is jeopardised to the point where it becomes a failure with serious ramifications: a broken leg; a wounded old lady; a ruined football season for the entire team.

A winner's primary motivation is one thing and one thing only: success. For that reason, winners will not do anything that might jeopardise success. I teach winners to realise that a critical situation is not the time to experiment and try out something new. We're not talking just about life-or-death scenarios, but anything that means a lot to us. When the margin for error is slim, an unproven method is too risky. Occasionally, the risk may pay off, and that may appear to justify taking it. But winners work with the laws of probability to increase the frequency of winning – and they will not tolerate pushing their luck by flirting with failure. Instead, winners keep to a very simple rule: in a crucial situation, they stick to what has been proven to work before – a parachute packaged the tried-and-tested way; a calm and soothing negotiating voice; a penalty placed accurately in the bottom left-hand corner.

This sounds logical and simple enough, but many people still fail because they don't stick to what works. Why? There are various reasons.

## A LACK OF AWARENESS OF WHAT WORKS AND WHAT DOESN'T

Of course, you have to know what works in the first place in order to be able to stick to it. If you're not aware of the correct, proven method, then it is going to be more difficult to replicate success. This shows the importance of continuous debriefing (see Chapter 4) in order to learn from your successes as well as from your failures. Otherwise there will be no consistency to your actions. Our negotiator, Sandra, knows from evaluating past experiences which tactics tend to work and those that definitely don't. If she had managed to debrief in real time, she might have salvaged her situation before it went wrong.

## THE EFFECT OF BOREDOM

'Boring, boring Arsenal.' This is what opposing fans would shout at Arsenal FC when they used to win the league by playing exactly the same way every week. Why did they do it? Because it worked time and time again. Now that Arsenal have changed their style to play much more exciting, varied and 'beautiful' football, the Arsenal fans sing it themselves as a self-referential joke. But the fact is, while they are undoubtedly better to watch these days, they are not as successful as they used to be. For some people, success is not the be-all and end-all; enjoyment is. Fine, and good for them. (This attitude is more acceptable in entertainment such as football; less so in serious business.) But for winners, winning is all that matters. Indeed, winning is the most fun, so they stick to what works like the warriors they are. Flamboyance and style are much lower on the list of priorities.

When people are bored or not stimulated enough, like John, they are often tempted to try something new. This is especially true with some very intelligent and highly skilled people as their boredom threshold can be low. So this is another reason why intelligence and skill can sometimes hinder success. Winners derive their enjoyment first and foremost from winning. For them, success is never boring.

Repetition often brings boredom with it. The more confident and comfortable you are in your own ability, the greater the temptation to veer from the script. It's human nature to want to experiment, to improvise, to try new experiences, to attempt to improve the process. But there is a time and a place to experiment – and it is not when the situation is critical.

In critical situations, such as those faced at work, you have to fight the strong urge to try something new 'just for the hell of it'. This reinforces what I said in the Introduction – that you don't need to be extremely clever to be a winner. Sometimes the less sophisticated thinkers are the most successful, because they are less tempted to experiment at the wrong time.

That's not to say that creativity and experimentation aren't important – of course they are, as we shall see later. But in critical situations, a winner is more disciplined to stick to what works, no matter how much temptation there is to try otherwise. Experiment in practice; deliver in performance.

## THE TEMPTATION TO SHOW OFF

Whether through overconfidence or a desire to impress someone and be seen as successful, people can get carried away and do something they wouldn't normally do. This is especially true in situations where people are afraid to lose face or respect in front of others. It might be that there is pressure to stay out drinking with work colleagues when you know you have a big meeting the following day. Or it could be that you don't want to back down and look weak to others in a confrontation situation and so end up dealing with it badly. This kind of peer pressure can cloud judgement, cause us to behave in an ill-advised manner and lead to regrettable results.

## THE EFFECT OF PRESSURE

Pressure does funny things to people's judgement as well as their performance. Just as the snooker player will choke on the black ball, or the mind of a highly intelligent person on a television quiz show will go blank on an easy question in the heat of the studio lights, so we can often let pressure get the better of us. When we panic, we are not thinking clearly and rationally. In fact, we might not be thinking at all. This means we are more likely to change the tactics that have been working perfectly well up until now – just like Anil when he was taking the penalty.

This is something I often have to work through with athletes and managers. They get into an advantageous position and then suddenly change the tactics that have been working perfectly well up until that point – and then everything unravels. They might try and protect an advantage by being more defensive; they might be even more aggressive to try and kill the game off; or they might get very nervous when they think they are about to win and 'choke' at the crucial moment because they don't know how to transform an advantage into a finite win. So they try something completely out of the blue. Suddenly changing proven tactics to something you haven't tried before when you are under pressure is rarely the right thing to do. The same is true in all spheres of life.

Of course, sometimes you want to try something different that your opponents will not be expecting in order to catch them off guard. But if you change what is working, you increase the likelihood of losing the advantage you already have and therefore bring in an element of unnecessary risk. If it is working, why change? In competitive situations you should change your proven working tactics only when you are absolutely sure your opponent has worked out how to combat them.

## THE OCCASIONAL FAILURE OF CORRECT TACTICS

This is where winning can get complicated. Sometimes the right tactics don't get the results they deserve. It might be that a promotion goes to a rival at work whom you know was a weaker candidate than you. Or it could be that a personal relationship fails through no real fault of your own. Or maybe the goalkeeper just got lucky for once. This is another example of the strength of debriefing in informing your method. It is only by debriefing thoroughly that you can realise whether or not you should stick to your tactics, despite this failure. You should rely on the evidence of past experience to dictate whether or not you change tactics. Don't allow emotions, feelings or intuition to rule over evidence. If, of course, the tactics should continue to fail more than they succeed, then you will need to change them. We'll come to how later in this chapter.

# ALL CHANGE PLEASE

All this talk of sticking to what works in critical situations – and resisting the temptation to experiment – would seem to stifle creativity, progress and improvement. It sounds like winners are very boring, robotic people, repeating the same things over and over again and never trying anything new. I can assure you that this is far from the case because winners are driven by a deep desire to develop continually.

*We are what we repeatedly do. Excellence, then, is not an act but a habit.*

In complete contrast to sticking to what works in critical situations, at all other times it is extremely important for winners to work at improving their methods. It's a process of trial and refinement, and this continuous development is what keeps humankind progressing in all spheres of life. If you're standing still, you'll find yourself going backwards as everyone else moves ahead. However, the creative improvement process needs to be approached in the winning way:

▶ At the right time: never in a critical situation when the existing method is working well.
▶ In the right way: while still adhering to the winning model and the winning behaviours of T-CUP.

In essence, this is precisely what you are doing in reading this book: experimenting with new ideas and methods; trying a new way of working in order to progress.

## TIME FOR PLAN B?

Winners don't put all their eggs in one basket. That in itself is a 'corner' – an unnecessary risk – and risks are anathema to winners. So at the initial stage of the winning behaviour cycle – creating the opportunity for the desired success – winners will work on developing a Plan B and Plan C. They will practise and perfect these contingencies until they are no longer at an experimental stage but ready to be used as the second step of the winning behaviour cycle – seizing the opportunity for the desired success.

So how do you come up with contingency plans? There are no hard-and-fast rules about boosting creativity – that's half the point of being creative – but here are a few suggestions that may help you think differently and come up with new ideas:

### Be positive and open

First things first – the winning mindset has to be right. Tell yourself that you can come up with great ideas; that you will figure this out. Boost your 'I will' power. Be open to new ideas. An atmosphere of openness is instantly more conducive to winning creativity.

## Focus

What are you trying to achieve? Aimless brainstorms tend not to be very productive. It might sound tautological, but you need to give the creativity session some boundaries in order to give it reason, direction, impetus and motivation.

## Let rip

Go for quantity, not quality, to start with. Come up with more ideas than you need so you have something to choose from. This forces you to think more widely; to think outside the box; to look at the problem from a different angle. Don't discriminate at this brain-storming stage – you can refine the ideas later. And you never know where one tangent might lead you...

## Speak up

Don't be afraid to express your creativity and your originality in group situations. So what if not every idea is brilliant. That's the same for everyone, winners included. This is a brainstorm and any not-so-good ideas can stimulate the generation of better ones. People respect those who respect themselves and have the gumption to participate. If feeling frustrated at your reluctance to put forward your ideas is your problem, deal with it like a warrior. Change to a winning mindset.

## Make a record

Give your memory a jog. There's nothing more frustrating than a great idea you can't remember. Try:

▶ writing down your ideas on a big sheet of paper or in a journal
▶ cutting things out of magazines and newspapers and adding them to a scrapbook
▶ adding to an open document on your computer

▶ recording ideas on a Dictaphone
▶ taking pictures of your ideas
▶ sending yourself an email when you have an idea.

## Come again

Force yourself to look at the problem from a different perspective: the man in the street, your client, a scientist, your grandmother, yourself in five years, James Bond. How would they think about it?

## Make time productive

Set aside a block of time to do nothing but think up ideas. Take the phone off the hook, switch off your mobile and computer to give yourself some head space. Then give yourself mini-deadlines: five minutes to come up with 10 ideas. Go!

## Get inspired

Stare out of the window, look at pictures, get out of the office or the house, take a shower, go and talk to someone different. Allow different stimuli to spark an idea – you never know when it might hit you.

## Talk it through

Sometimes just vocalising your thoughts can make them clearer because you have to make sense of the jumble in order to be able to explain it. Other people might give you a different perspective on your thoughts, ask pertinent questions or have great ideas of their own that you can develop together. Working with someone who thinks differently to you can be especially effective – a Sherlock Holmes to your Dr Watson, or vice versa. It might cause a few arguments, but creative arguments can produce good results.

## Work backwards

What's your desired end result? Work back from there by looking at the steps that are necessary to get to that point. This is also an effective way of keeping focused.

## Let it sit

Mull it over, let it ferment or stew a while. Then come back to the brainstorm afresh and see what you can add. That way you give your unconscious mind time to think it over.

# TO DO: What's the big idea?

Most people think creativity is a gift – you've either got it or you haven't. I believe it's a skill – the more you work at it, the better you'll get. So let's start practising.

1. Take a clean sheet of paper.
2. Think of a few things in your life that could do with freshening up. Perhaps work has got a bit formulaic; maybe you haven't changed your gym routine in a while; maybe your weekends are not very exciting. Jot as many of these things down as you like in the top left-hand corner of the sheet of paper, taking inspiration from your 'problem pages' in Chapter 1 if needs be. Try and come up with at least five.
3. Choose one item on that list and write it inside a bubble in the middle of the sheet of paper. For example: WEEKENDS.
4. Then, using as many of the suggested tips above as you want, brainstorm different plans. Allow yourself to go off at tangents. See what you can come up with in a set time, say 10 minutes. Then stop and look at what you've got.
5. Turn the sheet over and do the same for another item on your list and so on.

6. Look back at what you have produced and choose at least one idea worth acting on or developing. Then act upon it. Try it out in a non-critical situation and see how it works.
7. Debrief so that you can improve the creative process for next time.

## GET RID OF WHAT DOESN'T WORK

We're comfortable with the idea of 'if it ain't broke, don't fix it'. But if it is broken, then of course it does need fixing – and we shouldn't ignore it. By weeding out faults and problems, we will decrease our frequency of losing and therefore increase our frequency of winning. It's a very simple concept, and yet as we have seen before, it's amazing how many people continue to give themselves next to no chance of success by continuing to use methods that are proven time and again not to work.

Why? The reasons are varied, but you will be able to identify with all of them.

### BAD HABITS

We've all got them and it takes great self-awareness, discipline and winning warrior spirit to be able to kick them. Perhaps you're the kind of person who is useless with time and leaves everything until the last minute when it becomes a stressful panic (in which case, read Chapters 8 and 9). Or maybe you're not so good with money – and tend to spend freely at the start of the month when you've been paid, leaving yourself living in penury towards the end, waiting desperately for the next payday. Or perhaps you've allowed yourself to get your priorities wrong over time, concentrating less on life at home and more on work or socialising. We often know what we're doing is self-destructive, and it's up to us to find the self-discipline – the winning warrior spirit – to change. By debriefing, we identify and recognise bad habits as losing behaviours. Get rid of them.

## BAD CULTURE

You might do things in a certain way because this is how you were taught and the way things have always been done in your culture. An unhelpful culture is difficult to change – especially on an individual level – and that can make it all the more frustrating to deal with. This is especially true where too much emphasis is placed on tradition instead of moving with the times.

## BAD ATTITUDE

Often it's very difficult for us to admit our methods are wrong. It could be to protect our ego or reputation – we're determined to prove we are right. Or it could be that we have spent a lot of time, effort or money on the wrong method and are determined not to see that wasted, so we plough on pig-headedly. But if the method is clearly wrong, we are not doing ourselves any favours in sticking by it. To admit you're wrong when you are wrong is not a sign of weakness; it's actually a sign of strength, especially if you then move swiftly to put it right. If, through debriefing, we can face up to a mistake and not allow it to slow our momentum towards ultimate success, then that demonstrates the winner's strength of character.

# HOW TO DISCOVER WHAT DOESN'T WORK – AND WHAT TO DO ABOUT IT

Once more, we see the value of continuous debriefing. It's only by constantly evaluating your progress or otherwise that you can spot whether or not you are on track. The more you debrief (both during and after your task), the more likely you are to stay focused on the goal, and aware of what you need to do to meet it. Should you begin to veer off course, you are more likely to spot it sooner and correct it before the problem escalates. As the old adage goes, 'a stitch in time saves nine'.

So, how do you get yourself back on track?

1. Get **back to basics** (see page 77). Since your basics are your most up-to-date lessons from past experience, they are your safety net. Therefore, sticking to them is your default setting, almost like an autopilot. It will minimise damage while you figure out which steps to take next.
2. If, by debriefing, you conclude that Plan A is no longer effective, implement a tried-and-tested **Plan B**. This is a method you will have developed and perfected during non-critical situations (in rehearsal as opposed to performance).
3. **Debrief** continuously. When you apply your Plan B, evaluate its success. Is it producing the desired results? Could it be improved? How? If the new method appears to be more successful than the old method, then stick to it. Make it part of your 'basics'. Don't revert to the old one out of habit – stick to what is now working more effectively and refine it.

## STRIVE FOR THE BEST POSSIBLE RESULT

The single-mindedness of winners means that they strive for perfection and to give their personal best at all times. However, there needs to be a balance between perfectionism and practicality. You should strive for the best possible result in the time you have available. A winner will never go for second best unless, through circumstances, the second-best option becomes the best one. A winner's decision-making allows them to judge the best possible option. How do you make the right decisions? That is the subject of the next chapter…

# SEVEN

# HOW TO MAKE THE RIGHT DECISIONS

## GOALS

- ☑ to realise what kind of decision-maker you are
- ☑ to win the battle against procrastination – but know when to take your time
- ☑ to increase your sense of control over situations
- ☑ to improve your 'I will' power
- ☑ to make better decisions the winning way

## DECISIONS, DECISIONS

Three friends – Nick, Sanjay and André – have all been with their partners for about three years. They are in their late 20s, and other people in their social group have begun to get married and/or have kids. (One couple has even got divorced already.) All this has got the three friends thinking about their long-term plans. Is marriage right for their respective relationships? If so, when? If not, what's going to happen?

They each know that, together with their partner, they need to make a decision at some point about where the relationship is going – but there is no deadline on that decision as such.

Nick definitely wants to be with his partner for life but doesn't believe in the institution of marriage. After all, marriage is clearly not for everyone. Whenever the conversation has come up before, he has changed the subject. He thinks they are perfectly happy as they are – why change? But at one wedding reception, after a few drinks, his girlfriend asks him when he is going to get his act together and propose. They realise that they want different things, and now the entire relationship is in jeopardy.

Sanjay very much wants to get married – but he is scared. Scared of growing up and facing responsibility; scared of things not working out; scared of asking her father's permission; scared of being turned down; scared of having to take the initiative. Rather than face up to the situation, he would prefer just to let fate decide how things turn out. Now is not a great time as work is really hectic and they are busy with the house and everything. If it's meant to be, it will happen eventually. What's the rush? Whether through hesitation, procrastination or an inability to face a tough situation, Sanjay needs to be careful that he doesn't let the window of opportunity close on his fingers.

André has been thinking about getting married for a while. He's weighed up the pros and cons. There weren't really any cons. He's seen how happy his married friends are; he's subtly discussed the possibility with his girlfriend; he's been saving up money that could be used for a ring and a wedding. He's ready and he's sure – and what's more, he's pretty sure that she's sure. So he's planned a surprise weekend away in their favourite place next month when he's finally going to pop the question.

Three people, each with a life-changing decision to make, and each with a different approach to making that decision. Nick's decision not to get married but to keep things as they are may well be the right one for him ultimately, but not necessarily for his girlfriend. He makes the decision on her behalf without proper thought or consultation with his partner and, in terms of their happiness together, it backfires. He thinks he's in control but he's not. Sanjay would prefer not to make a decision at all. He doesn't want the control. He blames his indecision on external factors, and argues that it's not just up to the man to make decisions like this, and it's more romantic to keep things unplanned anyway. But will the window of opportunity stay open forever or will his girlfriend soon get bored, frustrated or tempted by someone with more drive in life? Unlike Sanjay (and Nick to a lesser extent), André is prepared to face up to the situation and make a rational and informed decision based on what he and his partner want. It might not seem very romantic or spontaneous, but he'll make it seem that way on their weekend away.

Who can say what the future holds for the three of them? But of the three, André is the one most in control. This has nothing to do with marriage and whether or not that denotes success. It's about André using the winning ways to minimise the risks and the uncertainty and therefore maximise his chances of happiness – and hopefully those of his fiancée too.

But let's speak of Nick's case: he was trapped between two poor options. None of these were good choices as far as he was concerned. This happens to everyone now and then because we do not live in an ideal world. That's life. So how can a winner make his decision under such circumstances? What decision will he or she take? A true winner will weigh up the alternatives to gauge what situation each decision will lead to, which decision will put them in less of a corner. If this fails, because none of the given options seems to have a significant advantage over the others, only then will winners go with their heart, their intuition. In most cases the decision they take – especially after weighing up alternatives – will prove itself to be the correct one.

This chapter is all about how to take control and make correct, clear decisions. Take the advice or leave it – the choice is yours.

## TO DO: What kind of decision-maker are you?

Think about a big decision that you need to make. Not what sandwich you should have for lunch today – something more important. Perhaps about a job, a place to live, a new business venture, a large purchase, a relationship. Now look at the 12 statements that follow and give each a rating out of 5 (where 1= not true at all, and 5 = exactly true).

1. I don't even need to think about that – the decision is obvious.
2. Why are you even asking me? You know what I always say.
3. I can't think about that right now – I've too much on my plate.
4. I'll tell you tomorrow.
5. Let me sleep on it.
6. What if I make the wrong decision?
7. What would so-and-so think?
8. Let's wait and see what happens.
9. Don't ask me – ask him.
10 I'm not sure – I keep changing my mind.
11. I'm very sure – my mind is made up.
12. I simply don't know how to make this decision.

If you scored highly on...

... 1, 2 or 11, you are DECISIVE/CONSISTENT.
But beware of making snap decisions or always making the same decisions without thinking them through according to the winning behaviours of T-CUP.

... 3, 4, 5 or 8, you are HESITANT/A PROCRASTINATOR.
As you are about to learn, sometimes it is okay to buy yourself more thinking time, but be careful not to delay your decision for too long or the window of opportunity may slam shut. Read on immediately!

... 7 or 9, you are NOT KEEN ON RESPONSIBILITY.
Asking others for advice is sensible, but don't rely on everyone else to make decisions for you. Winners are proactive, as this chapter will demonstrate.

... 6, 10 or 12, you are INDECISIVE.
But don't worry. You've come to the right place to learn how to be decisive the winning way. That's one thing you can be sure of.

# WHAT'S YOUR ANSWER TO EVERYTHING?

## JUST SAYING NO?

Saying no all the time isn't really making a decision – it's more of a defensive reflex; a poor form of self-protection from failure. Making a good decision should involve a thought process and evaluation in a frame of mind that is ready to meet challenges. But if you are the type of person who says no to every opportunity, then either you are not thinking about it very much, or you have a very negative, restrictive mindset. Either way, you are not debriefing from past experiences in a positive, winning manner and so you could be missing out on some great opportunities in life.

If you are the kind of person who makes mostly negative decisions, it could be an indication that you need to work on boosting your self-belief. If that is the case, go back to Chapter 3, which deals with building up self-confidence. Then try saying 'Yes!' once in a while. You might find that you:

▶ surprise yourself
▶ make new friends and new opportunities
▶ overcome fears and boost your confidence – and thus your success rate
▶ enjoy life and experience more happiness.

## ARE YOU A 'YES TO EVERYTHING' PERSON?

Saying yes to everything isn't really making a decision either – it's a reflex.

▶ Extreme optimists find it very difficult to make a decision. These people tend to see every option as a possibility, and thus find it impossible to choose one – a bit like the kid who wants every flavour in the ice-cream shop.
▶ Others might want to keep all their options open until the last possible minute rather than potentially 'miss out'.

A winner, on the other hand, understands that it is impossible to do everything and knows how to maximise their potential. People who try to do everything end up doing nothing very well. They can cause a lot of stress or upset for themselves or for those who have been let down as a result. This is particularly ironic if they said yes in the first place only because they hate letting down important people, like their boss or partner.

A winner knows the value of prioritising and committing. If you find yourself becoming stretched too thinly, reacquaint yourself with your overall target or aim. Maintain that focus and do only what is necessary to hit that target and maximise your potential. If you allow yourself to be distracted from your goal, you are less likely to achieve it.

If you are the type of person who always says yes to everything and suffers the consequences, try saying no for once. You might well find that it:

▶ increases your sense of dignity
▶ increases your sense of control over your life (the inner locus of control)
▶ boosts your self-esteem as you feel like less of a 'yes-man'
▶ gives you more time and energy for your priorities
▶ earns you much more respect from other people.

---

### Do you make excuses instead of decisions?

Pausing for thought is fine and often essential, but at some point you have to make a decision and be prepared for the consequences. If you tend to delay making a decision or find some way of avoiding having to make it, or continually make excuses for not doing something, then it could be that you need to boost your self-belief, to remind yourself that you have the ability and wherewithal to make decisions. An inability to make or commit to a decision also suggests a lack of focus. Some people believe that there is always a better solution out there, so they keep delaying the decision – until ultimately they jeopardise their chances of success. Turn again to your ultimate goal, employ T-CUP (always start by reminding yourself of the basics) and do not allow yourself to be deflected.

---

# WHEN IT'S OKAY TO HESITATE. MAYBE.

Needless procrastination is extremely unhelpful – but we'll deal with that later! However, sometimes it's okay to take your time: when there is no deadline pressure; when you know the situation will improve; when you need to find out more information; or when you feel that a period of reflection might help you solve a problem. Be wary of making snap decisions, especially about important matters. Being careful and giving decisions legitimate consideration is not procrastination; it's avoiding unnecessary corners. It's just taking a sensible amount of time to come to your rational verdict – like a jury with a lot of evidence to consider. Ask yourself: 'Is it wise to make this decision now?' Winners are experts in functioning under pressure – but they are even more impressive in the way they avoid any unnecessary pressure.

## SLEEP ON IT

Often just focusing on something else for a short time can help. Take your mind off it for a while – as long as you promise yourself that you're not just burying your head in the sand. Go for a run; play chess; call up an old friend to talk about something completely different; sleep on it; jump in the bath. You never know – you might have your own eureka moment of inspiration when you're not even thinking about it.

## STEP BACK

You can be too close to the situation, too entangled in the tiny detail, especially if you are emotionally involved with it. Like one of those computer-generated pictures that seem to be made of meaningless dots until a dinosaur or flying bird appears, it's only when you step back and look at the bigger picture from a different angle that the answer suddenly appears out of nowhere. So look at the problem from someone else's perspective. Get another person's opinion or go for a walk to think it through in a new way.

## COOL DOWN

Try never to make a decision when in a heightened state of emotion – whether that be very angry, very upset or very happy. Emotions can inhibit your ability to think clearly and rationally. Wait until you have calmed down before acting and making a decision. That way you can be more confident it is the right one. The more you debrief yourself, the more you will realise how emotional you can be.

---

### The pros and cons of pros and cons

People often find it useful to write their problem at the top of a blank sheet of paper and draw a line down the middle of it to list both the advantages and disadvantages of an important decision. This is like playing devil's advocate with your mind, forcing yourself to consider both sides of an argument fairly and to weigh up what matters more. It's an especially useful exercise when strong emotions are involved, and are threatening to overrule common sense. However, do not ignore your intuition. When it comes to life-changing decisions, a combination of heart and head is usually the winning balance.

---

# EVERYTHING YOU WANTED TO KNOW ABOUT PROCRASTINATION BUT HADN'T GOT AROUND TO ASKING

Returning a 'challenging' client's call, paying bills, sending Auntie Mavis a birthday card or topping up the petrol tank – we all know what it feels like to put something off until it's too late and we get ourselves in trouble. When it comes to life's big decisions, we're often even more adept at coming up with better things to do. Whether it's too much to think about, too much responsibility, too threatening or too awkward a situation, we'll find any excuse to be indecisive. The good news is that procrastination need not be a lasting character flaw – merely a bad habit you can change. Here's how.

The first stage of dealing with procrastination is being aware of it. So, debrief to raise your awareness of when, why and how you are doing it. See if you can spot yourself in some of the following common types of procrastination – then immediately follow the advice for dealing with it. Don't put it off till later.

## COMPLICATIONS OF COMPLACENCY

Complacency is anathema to winning. When it comes to decision-making, it might show itself in several forms:

▶ Overconfidence, giving the person the false impression that they are completely in control – 'There's plenty of time, I'll decide later.'
▶ A lack of care or concern – 'I can't be bothered right now.'
▶ Pure laziness – 'I'm too tired to think about it.'
▶ Naive optimism and underestimation of problems – 'That shouldn't take long.' 'It's easy.'

But just as the tortoise beat the hare, sometimes we can pay a big price for complacency. All of a sudden we run out of time, or unexpected complications sneak up on us – and what should have been very straightforward then becomes needlessly difficult or critical.

**Deal with it:** If it seems too easy or not stimulating enough, then refocus. Look at your ultimate desired success and use that desire to help you get on with the task in hand. Or make it more interesting –

perhaps by involving someone else to do it with you, or by listening to music or changing your environment temporarily. Perhaps enlist the help of a more proactive partner to help you draw up a to-do list and tick things off. Most importantly, think of the price you might pay. Learn from those occasions when your complacency cost you and vow never to repeat those mistakes again.

## FEAR OF FAILURE

Whether it's because we have too much of an ego (we don't want to be seen to fail) or too little (we don't know if we could handle the failure, and any mistake would be proof of our incompetence), fear of failure is what often stops people having a go in life. If the situation seems a bit daunting, we might just go missing. We won't volunteer or initiate; we won't put ourselves in the limelight; we'd prefer others took the responsibility. Some of us don't try, as if by not trying we have an excuse when things go wrong. We may think it's better to have failed without trying than to have failed when giving our best. This is a form of self-preservation that, ironically, performs the opposite function. Shoot for the stars and the sky is the limit. Shoot with no real aim and you're going to miss.

**Deal with it:** Success doesn't happen in a straight line. There will be setbacks, as we have already learned – but if you can learn from the failure it is still a very useful exercise, and should ensure you don't fail so much in future. All the best people make mistakes. It proves they are giving it a go; getting out of their comfort zone a bit; challenging themselves; stretching themselves. If you never failed, it would be proof that life is too easy, too boring, and you're not pushing yourself enough – like the skier who never falls over. Also, be assured that everyone fears failure to some extent – no matter who they are. The difference between winners and everyone else is the readiness to face those fears. How? By reminding yourself that while you can't excel at everything, you can significantly improve at anything if you want to. The learning curve just needs to be an upward one. Stop thinking in terms of 'I can't' and start boosting your 'I will' power. Follow the winning model of being a warrior, thinker and skill refiner. Practise, practise, practise, and keep on debriefing and you cannot fail.

## DODGING DISCOMFORT

Sometimes the less glamorous things we have to do in life seem like too much hard work. We don't want to tidy up the house, start that huge assignment, pay those bills, fill out that insurance form, send off that parking fine or plug away at the books. We don't want to do whatever it takes to create the opportunity for our desired success. Sometimes the things we are avoiding are more important, like facing up to money problems, dealing with a failing relationship or confronting a close friend who is messing up her life. Or it could be that the size of the task in hand feels too overwhelming and we don't even know where to start.

**Deal with it:** Break each task down into bite-size chunks. It might seem like a big job, but sometimes it's just a case of getting started – so start! Give yourself 15-minute blocks to get things done and tick them off as you go along. In just one well-planned hour you could draw up an agenda for a board meeting, set up a couple of direct debits, write a thank-you letter and arrange dinner with that friend you haven't had time to speak to in over a month. Or you could make the task more fun – get the kids to help you with the decorating; go to a nearby café for a brainstorm instead of the boring boardroom. Enjoy the satisfaction of getting things done – they won't be hanging over you any more. If you are finding the decision just too difficult to make, work backwards from your ultimate desired success. That can help you to focus. Be daring and go for it.

## MOOD BARRIERS

Sometimes we convince ourselves that, for whatever reason, the time isn't right. We can't think now. We've got too much stress. We're not in the mood. We just don't feel like it. We'll sleep on it. When how we feel dictates the timescale, productivity can go awry.

**Deal with it:** Think how much more stressed you will be later, how much more tired you'll be, how much more you will have on your plate if you delay it any further. Get on with it and you're more likely to improve your mood. Set yourself goals with rewards as long as you meet your targets. You can watch all the *Gardeners' World* you want once you've finished the washing-up. Think in terms of delayed gratification and how much better you will feel once it's done. Just like everyone else, winners suffer from bad moods and loss of motivation and interest. However, they develop a high pain threshold – mentally and physically – to help them fight against such internal obstacles. This is what winning is all about: no miracles, just being a warrior and a thinker.

## BUSY DOING NOTHING

These are the people who appear to be very busy, but don't actually seem to get an awful lot done. They spend forever planning, they fuss about how much they have to do but never start doing any of it. They also get easily distracted. When the house needs cleaning, they will spend hours rearranging their CD collection. They will sit in meetings every day but not decide on anything except to have another meeting about it. The irony is that they probably spend more time and energy not doing the task than it would have taken to get the thing done in the first place.

**Deal with it:** This problem is often due to a lack of self-awareness so listen if a friend or colleague points it out to you. Prioritise and set yourself realistic time barriers by which to achieve certain tasks.

Obviously, not everything can be done in 30-minute slots, but you can break big jobs up and build some momentum as you chip away at them. Scribble the tasks down on a Post-it in half-hour increments. And no, you don't need to spend forever colouring in the timetable. And no, you don't need to have a quick cup of tea first. The clock is ticking – get moving. At the end of the half-hour, move on to the next thing, no matter what. Keep debriefing and checking that you are making progress.

# HOW TO DECIDE LIKE A WINNER

The formula for making the right decision is all about increasing your RECOGNITION and AWARENESS. Use this easy 10-point plan.

## 1. SWITCH ON TO THE WINNING MODEL

▶ Turn your winning mindset back to the 'on' position – do not tolerate anything but a win.
▶ Remind yourself of the ultimate target in order to help you make your decision.
▶ Define your desired success by measurable parameters: 'I'll boost sales by 15 per cent by January…' 'I'll finish by 3pm…' 'I'll get to the end of the chapter…' 'I'll run 5km…'

Then use the winning model (noble warrior, thinker, skill refiner and continuous debriefer) to hit that target. For example: I want to pass that professional exam next month (WARRIOR and THINKER). Therefore I will stay in tonight (NOBLE WARRIOR) and revise (SKILL REFINER) and work on that subject I've been finding difficult recently (CONTINUOUS DEBRIEFER) rather than accepting that invitation to go to the pub. Renewing focus can renew momentum. Be a warrior from the start and fight against your shortcomings and any obstacles. Always keep your desired success at the forefront of your mind – it will help orientate you to make the correct decisions and stay on the right path.

## 2. SWITCH OVER

Figure out what kind of decision-maker you are – using the quiz at the start of this chapter if you haven't already done so – and resolve to make a plan to improve. Even someone who generally makes the right decisions can increase the frequency of those correct choices. 'Generally' can become 'usually' can become 'always'.

## 3. SET REALISTIC DEADLINES

When there is no set deadline, there is no pressure. This kind of flexibility can be dangerously unproductive. Put yourself under 'good pressure' by setting a realistic deadline by which to make the decision. Set targets and make them known to others to encourage yourself to stick to them.

## 4. KNOW YOUR ENEMY

When creating the opportunity for success, look at what your personal obstacles are, based on past debriefing. Stop and think about what is standing between you and success and resolve to bridge that gap. For example, reduce any uncertainty by proactively collecting information – making inquiries, learning the facts, perfecting skills, consulting experts, discussing possibilities, evaluating options. Make sure your decisions are well-informed. No one can expect to feel 100 per cent certain when making a decision, but you can minimise the unknown element, thus reducing the potential for a wrong decision. Winners don't like to take uncalculated risks as these are typical 'corners', so they weight the risks in their favour by reducing the amount of uncertainty, controlling as many variables as possible. Avoiding unnecessary risks is winning behaviour. This means that you can be confident of having made the best possible decision.

## 5. KNOW YOURSELF

Trust your intuition. If, after a rational evaluation following T-CUP and assessing the corners, your gut instinct strongly tells you to go one way, then it's probably the right way. Intuition is truly an 'educated guess' because it is based on a lifetime's accumulated experience, so it should not be underestimated or ignored.

## 6. KNOW YOUR OWN MIND

It's advisable to seek the advice and counsel of others, especially experts, but don't allow anyone else to dictate your actions or force you into a decision you are not happy with. Sometimes we second-guess what people will think – such as our parents or our boss – and act according to their expectations of us, or to try and please them. Guilt, the weight of expectation and a sense of powerlessness can all sap us of our decisive energy. But again, make sure you agree with every decision you make. Remind yourself what your ultimate desired success is and use that as your guide or motivation.

## 7. TURN FEAR INTO FUEL

Be a warrior. Don't allow fear to be an inhibitor that dictates your decisions. Treat it as a challenge rather than as a barrier. In a similar way to people who find roller coasters or scary films fun, getting outside your comfort zone can be enjoyable, and it can help you learn about yourself. Doubt is natural and useful: it helps us make sure we are not making a thoughtless mistake. Use doubt to ensure that you double-check. This is not wasting time – in most cases it's a fantastic time-saver and it helps us achieve the best possible results.

A great weapon against fear is knowledge. Research your decision as far as possible. Gather as much information as you can and consult experts.

## 8. MAKE THE DECISION

Don't waste time and energy worrying about what might go wrong. Don't wait for other people or fate to make the decision for you. Be positive and proactive. Following all these rational steps, you are now ready to make the right decision. But it doesn't end quite there...

## 9. DEBRIEF YOUR DECISION

Having used the appropriate winning behaviours to reduce uncertainty and error, don't be afraid to continually evaluate whether or not you made the right decision. (For a quick recap of the winning behaviours, see the box overleaf.) A quick stitch in time can save nine. If you feel you have made a mistake, change it rather than carry on. Too many people carry on along the wrong lines either through a lack of awareness through not debriefing, or because it feels easier or less embarrassing to stick to their guns. However, living with the consequences of a bad decision will always cost you a lot more than switching to the right decision as soon as possible. A continuous debrief means you are unlikely to have strayed too far down the wrong path. Always go for the best rewarding decision, even if that is not necessarily the easiest one.

## 10. FOLLOW UP YOUR DECISION

Being able to make the right decision is brilliant, but it is not enough without action. Thinking like a winner means a rapid yet controlled transition from making the right decision to acting on it. To refresh your memory on how to put winning methods into practice, go back to Chapter 4.

**Need a quick recap?**

Remind yourself of those winning behaviours once again:

1. Avoid unnecessary corners
2. Create the opportunity
3. Seize the opportunity
4. Maintain the momentum
5. Strive for the best possible result
6. Stick to what works
7. Give up what doesn't work
8. Get back to basics
9. Improve your self-control
10. Make the correct decisions
11. Learn to thrive under one-on-one pressure
12. Maximise your use of time

# WHAT'S THE WORST THAT COULD HAPPEN?

We all imagine the worst from time to time, especially when contemplating life's big decisions. Blundering in without thinking or imagining possible consequences would be unnatural and unwise. But what is unhelpful is if you let your imagination get the better of you – to the point where you stick with the status quo and thus possibly miss out on the opportunity of a lifetime. Windows of opportunity don't stay open forever. Whether it's asking someone to marry you, applying for a job you're not sure you're qualified for or running a marathon, don't allow irrational fears to limit life fulfilment.

When faced with a big decision, it can actually be helpful to face up to and visualise how you would deal with the worst-case scenario for a number of reasons:

▶ If the worst should happen, you will be prepared for it, so it's actually less daunting.

▶ You will come up with a plan of action to ensure it never gets to a disastrous stage.

▶ You will realise that the likely outcome is actually not nearly as bad as your overactive imagination might think.

But instead of focusing on what can go wrong and worrying about it, focus on what can go right, how you can make it happen and think about how satisfying that would be. Psychologists realise the power of positive visualisation: picture the deal going through; picture getting a round of applause; picture your offer being accepted... Visualise the success and aim for it. Ultimately the best way to deal with an irrational fear is to focus on what is in your control:

▶ how you feel

▶ how you can get back to what works when you lose focus or get distracted

▶ how you can put plans in place to increase your chances of success and decrease your chances of failure

▶ how it feels when you achieve and succeed.

Too many people continue with a wrong decision because they feel that otherwise the preparation and hard work that led up to that decision is a waste, and to save themselves from the frustration of admitting that they were wrong. However, it's important to set aside procedures that don't work and don't bring the desired results, and embrace new behaviours and processes. You don't want to pay for your mistakes twice.

**THINK: How to make a big decision**

Next time you face an important crossroads in life, ask yourself the following list of questions, as appropriate:

1. What is my ultimate desired aim?
2. What motivates me to want that?
3. What could be a benefit and a possible corner?
4. What is your criteria to measure your success?
5. What are the consequences if you achieve success?
6. What are the consequences if you fail?
7. What do I need to know to get a better idea of the likely outcome, and how could I get that information?
8. What are the practical alternatives?

# IT'S UP TO YOU

Just as you can choose to think differently if you put your mind to it, so you can decide to make better decisions if you want to. If you follow the advice in this chapter, I guarantee that your choices will start to improve. The decision is yours.

# EIGHT

# HOW TO HANDLE PRESSURE

## GOALS

- ☑ to manage and reduce pressure through control
- ☑ to use stress positively
- ☑ to reduce and prevent stress through thinking and acting differently
- ☑ to learn how best to deal with competitive and non-competitive one-to-one situations
- ☑ to learn how to cope outside your comfort zone

## YOU MUST BE CHOKING

The captain of industry who suddenly loses his nerve just as he is about to complete the biggest deal of his life; the tennis player who inexplicably crumbles at match point; the talented student who messes up her finals; the best man who forgets his well-rehearsed speech. Pressure can do funny things to us. When there's no pressure, we amble along, not really firing on all cylinders. Then, when we need to perform, the adrenaline kicks in and we can do really well. But when the pressure mounts too much and we realise what is at stake, the occasion can get to us and we can mess everything up.

---

## THINK: Nervous?

Think of an occasion in the past when you really needed to perform, but nerves got the better of you. Perhaps it was in an exam or a driving test; perhaps it was while giving a speech or a presentation; maybe it was while trying to chat someone up in a bar or sell yourself in an interview. Or maybe it was just when you missed an 'easy' black while playing pool recently...

## How does it make you feel?

In this chapter we are going to look at how winners can better handle pressure – something we have to cope with on a day-to-day basis, even if we try and avoid it.

---

# THE DIFFERENCE BETWEEN STRESS AND STRAIN

Chill out. Relax. Unwind. De-stress. Calm down. Lighten up. In today's hectic world, we're constantly being told to take it easy: whether it's to have a massage, drink some strange tea or take a deep breath and count to Zen.

Stress is perceived by most people to be a bad thing. I disagree. Psychologists acknowledge that a certain amount of stress is required to create the necessary arousal that helps us perform at our peak. Stress is great, if you know how to use and control it. Whenever we get a bit stressed or nervous, we are normally advised to relax. However, that could occasionally have a negative impact on our performance level, so it could be the entirely wrong action to take.

Athletes are often caught using performance-enhancing drugs, but nature provides the best performance enhancer of all: adrenaline. We need it to help us fulfil our potential. Adrenaline kicks in naturally when we need it, when we're under pressure or excited, and if we can learn how to harness its power, we can achieve great things – we can be winners. But like any drug, you can overdose on it or get addicted to it. That's when we talk of 'adrenaline junkies' and people on 'power trips'. And that's when it could cause you problems.

In order to understand how managing pressure can turn us into winners, we need to look at our stress levels and identify where we fit in.

## TO DO: Take the stress test

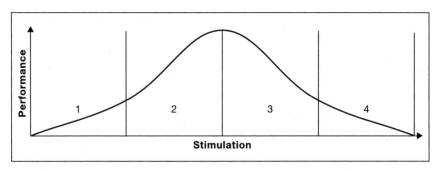

### Level 1: underworked
Relax. This is considered by many people to be the ideal state. There are no problems here; no pressures; no worries. Life is easy. Too easy, in fact. People at this level are not stimulated and so are not stretching or challenging themselves enough. The motivation is low so the performance level is low. Life is slowly passing them by and their potential remains unfulfilled. Where there is no stress, there is no progress.

## Level 2: working hard

Great – this is the optimum stress level, resulting in the best performance. Time flies when you're this excited, determined, alert and ready for action. It's a much more productive and active stage. The adrenaline is kicking in, but the nerves are under control. In fact, everything is under control. If only life could always be like this.

## Level 3: overworked

Things are getting a bit tough now. There's too much to do and not enough time to do it. Everything is beginning to get on top of you and you're worried you're not coping. You're starting to fray at the edges as you gradually lose control of the situation.

## Level 4: wrecked

At this stage, everything feels like a complete disaster. It's all gone wrong and there seems to be no way out of this mess. You don't know what to do first. You've totally lost control and you're extremely unhappy, panicked and stressed out. The stress spreads to other parts of your life too – it's all too much to cope with, your life is unravelling fast and you feel there's nothing you can do about it.

## What level are you at?

Chances are, we've all experienced life at every level at some point. The aim, of course, must be to make level 2 the norm. This is the only stage at which we can be winners, and where we can fulfil our true potential. If we're working hard then there will naturally be times when we slip into level 3 and things get a bit much for us. But as long as this is a temporary state of affairs and we get back into level 2 as soon as possible, that's okay. (Otherwise, things could escalate, and before we know it we're entering the dangerous realms of level 4.) Likewise, we might have a holiday in level 1 every now and then, just to recharge the batteries and take a breather. But we shouldn't get too comfortable there – or we might never get up again.

The good news is that, wherever you are currently, you can do something about it to make sure you get in level 2 and stay there – using the techniques in the rest of this chapter. Just knowing you are not powerless to sort it out will probably ease the stress a little straight away.

# DEALING WITH ONE-TO-ONE SITUATIONS

People who don't like pressure tend not to enjoy having to confront situations on their own. There's safety in numbers: you can hide behind other people, or at least draw strength and support from their presence. But the fact is that one-to-one situations are inevitable and unavoidable. The sooner we face up to them, the sooner we can start to turn them to our advantage.

These are all common one-to-one situations, though you might not think of them in such terms:

▶ disciplining your child
▶ reporting in to your boss
▶ bargaining with a stall-holder
▶ playing tennis against a friend
▶ negotiating with a client
▶ arguing with your partner
▶ rebuffing a persistent salesman
▶ asking for a pay rise
▶ defending yourself from hostile criticism.

Once you realise how often you face these situations, the more you appreciate the need to develop a strategy for dealing with them more effectively.

However, it is important to distinguish between competitive and non-competitive one-to-one situations, as each requires different treatment. One of the biggest mistakes people make is to confuse the two, or fail to distinguish between them and use the same tactics for both. When getting involved in a one-to-one situation you must take a brief moment to raise your self-awareness and evaluate what type of situation you are dealing with. Get this wrong, and your chances of winning are seriously jeopardised.

▶ **Competitive one-to-ones** are win–lose situations. For that reason, they require a more combative and assertive approach. Being too 'nicey-nicey' would probably be disastrous. The key is to undermine the other person's self-confidence and thus their performance. Do that successfully and they'll do the rest for you.
▶ **Non-competitive one-to-ones** are all about co-operation, collaboration and agreements. These are win–win situations. Being confrontational in such scenarios would more often than not be catastrophic. The key is to build up the other person's confidence in themselves, but most importantly in you, in your intentions and in the benefits of working with you.

Depending on our natural personality, we will tend to lean more towards one approach than the other. Competitive and dominant personalities will favour all-out war, while more sensitive or passive types will try and avoid confrontation at all costs. The key here is to read the situation straight away and adapt your behaviour accordingly.

## WE COME IN PEACE

In non-competitive one-to-one situations you need someone's co-operation, agreement or approval. Examples of such situations include:

▶ job interviews
▶ salary negotiations
▶ discussions with potential business partners
▶ meetings with a client, member of the public or your mother-in-law.

Often a compromise will be necessary. For some overly aggressive, competitive or egotistical people, the word 'compromise' is not in their vocabulary, and this is why they turn every one-to-one into a competitive situation. Put aggression and ego to one side here: compromise is a key issue in these situations. They are not about conceding ground or power; they are about working together to get what both sides want.

Here's how to deal with non-competitive one-to-ones:

1. Create the right mindset and accept that you need the other side to achieve success. Never be aggressive or domineering. Focus on your ultimate goal and use it to help you maintain self-control.

2. Use open and non-threatening body language. Smile – the most effective body language possible. Speak to people on their level: if they are sitting down, you sit down too. Try not to cross your arms or legs and ensure you maintain eye contact. These are classic body language techniques because they are proven to work.

3. Give the other person credit and respect to build up their self-confidence. Butter them up a bit, stopping short of being too obsequious.

4. Use empathy and positive language. Instead of saying, 'I completely disagree with you, you are totally wrong', try 'You are probably right – may I just add...' Instead of 'You don't understand', try 'Sorry, I didn't explain myself very well...'

5. Listen. Don't be too domineering and don't assume you know what the other person is thinking. Ask them and learn about them.

6. Be prepared to compromise. Admit it: you need the other side's co-operation. So show that you are ready to meet them part-way.

7. Continuously debrief. Make sure your tactics are helping you achieve your aim. If not, modify them.

## FIGHT, FIGHT, FIGHT!

In competitive one-to-one situations you need to gain an advantage, exert power over an opponent or literally defeat the other side. This is where you do need to find an element of controlled aggression and self-serving assertiveness – a mean streak – even if it goes against your natural instincts. Examples include:

▶ some business ventures and deals
▶ confrontations
▶ the sporting arena
▶ perhaps visits from the mother-in-law too!

It is amazing how often winners adopt the same strategy when it comes to a competitive scenario: invariably they target their opponent's self-confidence and seek to undermine it.

Think about it. How do you feel when your self-confidence is shot to pieces? How easy is it to draw upon your talents, skills or intelligence? In the moment of truth it really doesn't matter how skilled or clever you are if you are unable to utilise it. So the less confident your opponent feels, the less effective they will be.

As competitive one-to-ones are often very intimate, confidence is like the water in a water bed. Every shift in self-confidence causes an immediate change in the power levels. Apply pressure and see the result. And you will absorb any of the self-confidence your opponent is losing, which will push your performance up. Effective pressure is therefore a key issue.

# HOW TO WIN IN ANY SITUATION

## WHEN YOU'RE WINNING...

Once you've got the advantage, don't stop – exploit it. Don't get too excited and pleased with yourself and think you've won before you have; complacency is the scourge of winners. And if you suddenly get nervous when you think you're about to win, relax. You don't need to do anything other than what got you to that point. Don't change tactics or experiment. If it ain't broke, don't fix it. Winners know to stick with what works and drive the advantage home until they have won. That is the winning way. If your tactics are working, that means the opponent doesn't know how to deal with them. Push aside any fears that your opponent will discover your winning tactics. Your ongoing debriefing will help here, so you can deal with it as and when it happens.

## WHEN IT'S A DRAW...

This is a test of nerve. Be patient and persevere. Don't be tempted to change tactics unnecessarily as this could jeopardise your position and hand the advantage to your opponent. Don't allow your nerves, frustration or impatience to get the better of you. Keep focused on your ultimate goal of winning and maintain the self-control to apply the same type of pressure on your opponent using the same methods. The first one to blink will lose. Stick with it and you will emerge victorious.

## WHEN YOU'RE LOSING...

If you're the one under pressure or at a disadvantage, then you need to know how to get out of that situation quickly. The common response to pressure is to retreat, go on the back foot and be defensive. This is the reaction your opponents want to get from you so they can make ground. However, winners try never to adopt that defensive position when under pressure. Resist the natural temptation to be defensive. Counter the pressure with pressure. How do you know what effective pressure is? Debrief. Are you sticking to the basics? Are your tactics at fault? Be honest – winners don't stick slavishly to faulty methods. If necessary, change tactics the winning way. This doesn't mean you should experiment; it means reverting to a tried-and-tested Plan B or Plan C (see page 112). If you do all this in a controlled manner, and if you take the time to think despite the pressure (remember, under pressure we have more time than we feel we have), you'll be able to make a winning comeback – often against all odds. This is what Liverpool FC did when they came back from 3–0 down against AC Milan in the 2005 Champions League final. And this is what makes a winner.

# UNDER PRESSURE? THINK AGAIN

Pressure tends to make people act without thinking. That's why meeting pressure with pressure is such an effective tactic. If you can limit the time your opponent has to think and to act, then you will benefit from their unnecessary mistakes. You'll also buy more time for yourself and reduce the pressure you are under, enabling you to enjoy better performance and rate of success.

Acting without thinking vastly decreases chances of success. As we now know, the umbrella title for the winning behaviours is T-CUP: Thinking Correctly Under Pressure. Thinking is often perceived as a time-consumer, so people tend to forget it when the pressure is on.

Wrong! How often have you made a mistake when you've been put on the spot and 'haven't had time to think'? Intuition and instinct are not as reliable as rational thought. They can help inform rational thought, but they should not be a substitute for it.

Winners know that when they are under pressure, they always have more time than they feel they have. They also know that when they are under pressure, that is the time to think – especially as other people won't be doing it. (There, you have the advantage over them already.) You don't have to spend forever conducting a huge analysis. It might be as simple as refocusing on the relevant T-CUP rule. This takes no more than a split second. If you've only got a few seconds, you could refer to a cue card in your pocket; or if you have a couple of minutes you might come up with a quick three-point plan (perhaps with colleagues) of what needs to be done. Acting with thought can save you a huge amount of wasted time and effort if it cuts down on the chances of making mistakes and ending in failure. Therefore, thinking is always a great use of time.

## STILL THINK YOU'RE UNDER PRESSURE? THEN CHANGE YOUR MIND

We all respond to situations in different ways, often depending on our perception of the stress or pressure level. For instance:

▶ some people revel in exams; others fall apart in them
▶ some people like taking things easy and relaxed; others get bored and frustrated
▶ some people get off on roller coasters (both literal and metaphorical); others prefer just to get off them
▶ some people love to be centre of attention; others would prefer to be anywhere else
▶ some people thrive when they're really busy; others suffer meltdown.

A person who has to get up in front of 100 people and do a speech might fret about it for weeks, lose sleep, sweat on stage, stutter and stumble over their words, and generally make a right hash of it. But once they've done 100 such speeches, they won't be so nervous and so will have more control over the situation. Psychologists recognise that the way we view a situation makes a big difference to how we perform. They call it cognitive appraisal. So by changing the way we think about a situation, we can change the way we perform.

How do you change the way you think when the situation becomes really stressful and the pressure seems to get the better of you? Very simple: rather than thinking of how bad the situation is, direct your thoughts to searching for effective ways to improve the situation. Start looking for practical ways to turn the whole situation around, to find something productive and purposeful to do. That's being a warrior. That's having a winning mindset. And for doing it effectively, just go back to T-CUP.

Despite suffering from the same doubts and crises of confidence that we all experience from time to time, winners resist the tendency to foresee only the worst-case scenario. That would be tantamount to admitting that they are powerless to change the situation, a notion winners would find offensive. Instead, they mobilise their winning optimism and drive to find a winning solution. So simply by resolving not to give in, to be more in control, to be more confident in our abilities to deal with any sort of problem, to take the bull by the horns, we can dramatically improve. Shying away is much less likely to bring about success.

Winners are also able to think positively because they have prepared thoroughly. Therefore, they are not hoping for the best and relying on luck; they are expecting the best and relying on their ability to control the situation.

Next time you have to step outside your comfort zone, give yourself the following checklist.

### Give yourself credit

Rather than dwell on past bad experiences, remember when things have gone well and use that experience to gee yourself up. Don't attribute your successes to luck or fate – recognise your talents and ability and concentrate on replicating those successes. Don't take yourself for granted.

### Give yourself a pep talk

Most of us love it when people build us up and encourage us. It does great things for our confidence. Positive self-talk can do the same job, helping push out any negative and unhelpful thoughts. Say, 'Come on, I can do this... keep going... great work... I'm ready... I'm going to show them what I'm made of...' Use the language of T-CUP as well. For example, 'Counter the pressure with pressure... I need to get back to basics... I'm going to stick to what works...'

### Give yourself a breather

When you feel yourself getting too tense, take a moment to take a deep breath and compose yourself. Consider your next move and your best use of time.

### Give yourself a break

Recognise what you can do and take it one step at a time. If you've got a mountain of work to do or a huge problem to solve, don't waste time worrying about it. Make a start and build on it. If your team is 3–0 down, metaphorically speaking, concentrate on getting it back to 3–1, not 3–3. Just go step by step. You can only do your best – just make sure you do.

### Give yourself the best possible chance

Prepare and practise as much as you can. Reduce risk by controlling and mastering as many variables as possible.

### Give yourself control

Focus on what you can control, not what you cannot, by following the rules of T-CUP. Your behaviour and attitude are two things you can always control if you want to. Start with those and the rest will fall into place.

### Give yourself a pat on the back

Facing up to situations outside your comfort zone helps to keep you learning and growing as a person. It's not easy to start with, but you'll feel a real sense of achievement after completing something you didn't think you could accomplish. Make sure that you set yourself realistic challenges and that you congratulate yourself and enjoy the achievement.

### Give yourself feedback

That debriefing stage again. What did you do right? How exactly did you get it right? What could you have done better? How will you improve on it for next time? Work by trial and refinement, not trial and error.

# HOW TO STEADY YOUR NERVES

Nerves are tricky little blighters to control. When the heart begins to race and we start to feel the prickle of sweat, the tension in our body inhibits performance. The pressure is normally down to one or a combination of the following variables. Deal with them and ease the tension.

## THE TIME FACTOR

'I've run out of time!' When we feel we don't have enough time to complete something, we can start to panic. Winners know that they always have more time than they feel they have. So start by reminding yourself of it and you will instantly feel more relaxed.

Time management is the subject of the next chapter so we will deal with this issue in more detail then (see page 161). Remember, though, that however much time you've got – even if it's only a split second – winners have the rules of T-CUP to rely on. This helps them always make the optimum use of the time available. Use time pressure as a catalyst for action rather than as a catalyst for panic.

## THE COMPETENCE FACTOR

'Can I do this?' Negative thoughts are hugely influential at the moment of truth. If we have a sudden crisis of confidence and begin to doubt ourselves, we will probably mess up. Psychologists use CBT – cognitive behavioural therapy – to deal with these situations, or confidence-boosting techniques, as I like to call them. Winners are able to change automatic negative thoughts ('I'll never make it, it's too hard') into performance-enhancing thoughts ('Yes, I can do it and I will do it!'). This is exactly what changing your mindset is all about. Make it a habit. Other winning techniques include visualisation – mentally rehearsing everything going well. Preparing thoroughly will also increase your self-confidence. Believe that you can do it and that you have done everything possible in accordance with T-CUP to make it happen, and your chances of success are greatly enhanced.

## THE CONSEQUENCE FACTOR

'What's going to happen if I mess this up?' The fear of failure is a subject we touched on in Chapter 3 (page 60). As soon as people think of the consequences – whether it's winning a world cup or getting a big promotion – the focus is lost. Always use T-CUP to combat all kinds of negative thinking and control your nerves, your thoughts and hence your performance. Ultimately, the best way to avoid the worst is to focus on achieving your best by concentrating on what you can control:

▶ your mindset
▶ your plan
▶ your skills
▶ your ability to maintain focus and get back to basics if you ever find yourself distracted from your ultimate goal of winning.

Press the reset button rather than the self-destruct button.

---

## Be a model winner

Here's how the winning behaviour model can be used to help you cope with pressure:

### 1. Be a warrior

The first battle in handling pressure is with yourself. You have to fight against the natural tendency to act without thinking when you're under pressure, or to go on the defensive when someone attacks you. You have to be a noble warrior, the characteristic that underpins the whole winning philosophy (see page 14). Noble warriors constantly fight against negative thinking. They work hard, diligently and with great courage, self-control and discipline to overcome all sorts of internal and external obstacles. This means working according to the winning principles of T-CUP to raise their performance level so that they can exert more pressure on the opposition – sometimes against all the odds.

---

## 2. Be a thinker

In order to be an effective warrior, a winner has to be a smart one. Not smart as in 'intelligent', but smart as in 'using their head'. This means thinking even when under pressure in accordance with T-CUP. No one can fulfil their potential without thinking. It helps winners stick to their basics, avoid unnecessary corners and problems, and it ensures that their hard work is not a waste of energy.

## 3. Be skilled

Winners know that there is nothing they cannot improve at if they work at it. Having committed to working hard and in a thinking manner, winners are able to raise their skill level by practising. Successful people are successful because they work hard at developing and improving their performance, leaving as little as possible to chance. It might look like innate skill or talent, but that's because they have raised their pain threshold – mentally and physically – to put in the hard work the right way behind the scenes.

## 4. Be a continuous debriefer

At all times and at all stages – debrief.

# COPING WITH STRESS: EASY NOW

Easing the stress makes coping with it a lot more bearable. Three people are travelling back to London after business trips in New York. When they arrive at JFK airport, they see that their flight has been cancelled due to a technical fault with the plane.

James is irate. All he wants to do is get home. He's paid a lot of money for his business class flight. He doesn't care what the problem is – they have to get him home. He wants to see his family, he wants to sleep in his own bed, and he has to be back in the office for an important meeting the following day. So he shouts at the airline representative at the customer services desk. Then he shouts at the rep's boss. He makes himself extremely hot under the collar and unpopular. In the end, James accepts a seat on a later flight, but while he was busy arguing, all the spare seats went. So now he has to fly back in economy class via a stopover. Typical. The airline will be hearing about this! His attitude is to challenge a bad situation.

Ellen isn't exactly happy either but, as there's little that can be done about it, she resolves to make the best of the situation. She allows the airline to book her on a flight for the following day and sends her boss an email to explain that she'll be out of the office for a bit longer. Then she accepts the airline's offer of a taxi back to the hotel they are paying for and treats herself to a day's enforced holiday: doing the shopping she didn't have time for, and having a relaxing spa treatment. Bliss. Her attitude is to make the best of a bad situation.

This has happened to Mina before – and that time she managed to get the airline to fly her home on one of their partner carrier's planes. So while everyone else waits in a long queue to be told what to do, she goes to the business lounge and gets the phone number of the airline supervisor. Ten minutes and a sob story later, she's managed to negotiate a flight that night with another airline that arrives only a few hours after she was due back. She even gets an upgrade to first class. Bonus. Her attitude is to resolve a bad situation.

Three reactions to the same problem. James loses his cool and ends up losing out. He's proactive, but not positive. He allows himself to get very stressed, which ends up being a waste of energy and time, delaying him further. Ellen resolves to look on the bright side and ends up having a perfectly nice time – though she probably didn't need to buy both pairs of shoes from Barney's. She's positive but not proactive. Mina is positive and proactive, efficient and manipulative. Always calm in a crisis, she found herself a very agreeable solution.

The chances are we've all reacted to similar situations in similar ways in the past. We probably didn't even consider what the best strategy would be – we just did what felt right at the time, whether that was shouting, taking a back seat and letting it work itself out or trying to find a sneaky solution. But if we learn through debriefing 'what can I do better next time?', our success rate will rocket. As I said earlier, relying on intuition alone is a risky business. Give your instincts the following options so that the next time you're in a fix, you can fix it.

## THINK DIFFERENTLY

### Be your own editor

Newspaper editors are very skilled at spinning stories to suit their agendas. A sensationalist tabloid scandal could be lauded as a triumph in a broadsheet – it just depends on how you look at it. The same principle could be applied to your stressful situation. You can lose your cool and start to panic and achieve nothing. But a winner would choose to make the best of it like Ellen and enjoy the benefits. It doesn't mean that winners never get stressed or nervous – of course they do. They just deal with it more effectively and more positively. Winners believe instinctively that for any challenging situation there is a solution and they will always strive to find that solution. It's yet more proof that optimism is more effective than pessimism.

### Get some perspective

One thing goes wrong and our world collapses. Psychologists call it emotional reasoning – which sounds almost like a contradiction in terms. But look at the bigger picture. Does missing this flight really matter? Does splitting up with your partner mean that the world is going to end? It might seem like that for a while to start with – and understandably so – but think about what else is going right in your life. Maybe you've got a good job and friends and family that love you; your football team is in the cup final; you're going on holiday next month... It does you no harm to remind yourself of life's plus-points every now and then, especially when you're feeling low. Winners will always see the light at the end of a tunnel; losers will always believe that it is just a train coming towards them.

## ACT DIFFERENTLY

### Find a solution

By getting things done you are better able to cope, and by coping you are better able to get things done. Winners debrief constantly, which helps them find solutions all the time. Success isn't down to talent, IQ or bank account. It's just that where others give up, winners persevere. Winners don't just see the light at the end of the tunnel; they illuminate the whole thing. Be a winner, be proactive, draw up an action plan or talk to your friends to help brainstorm an answer to the problem. Then enjoy the satisfaction of achievement. By learning to cope more and more, winners develop trust in themselves; they build up self-belief and therefore a tolerance to stress and pressure which makes them better able to deal with it in the future.

### Have a break

Sometimes a temporary change of subject or scenery is just what's needed. You can't solve problems by running away from them forever, but a bit of head space can help you see things afresh. Go for a run to think it over. Go on holiday to forget about it. Go to bed to sleep on it. Then come back ready to deal with it.

The winning solution is a combination of thinking and acting differently. But the key thing to remember is not to blunder in without thinking first.

## Prevention is better than cure

Rather than waiting until we get really stressed out, wouldn't it be better to ward off the problem beforehand? We all know when we're getting stressed. It might be that we find it hard to get off to sleep, or we go off our food. It could be that we get really tense or suffer from headaches. We might get a bit snappy and easily frustrated. Be honest with yourself and, through debriefing, identify what your personal warning signs are. When you feel them coming on, take preventative action.

Also, after debriefing, work out how you could modify your behaviour and your habits to take the stress out of life. Perhaps you should get yourself a work and social diary and make sure you look at it to see when it's getting overcrowded. Or you could resolve to keep your financial records in better order by filing away your bank statements, setting up direct debits for bills and so on. Wherever your areas of weakness, look into ways of offsetting the problems.

## TO DO: It's your turn to deal

Think about a stressful or pressurised situation you've faced in the last six months:

1. How did you deal with it?
2. Having read the winning advice in this chapter, did you deal with it well?
3. How could you have dealt with it better?
4. What bad habits could you edit out in future to decrease your frequency of losing, despite the pressure?

Think about a potentially stressful or pressurised situation that you've got coming up:

1. What steps could you take now to help limit the stress and pressure you feel?
2. How will you deal with any stress and pressure when it comes?

3. What techniques can you adopt as helpful habits for the future to increase your frequency of winning, despite the pressure?
4. Write down your plan or strategy so that you can implement it, and then evaluate its level of success.

## LEARN TO LOVE THE JOY OF STRESS

Pressure is not something you can afford to shy away from. Like a novice skier about to embark on a challenging slope, sometimes you've just got to go for it. If circumstances allow, deal with it gradually. Be strong, be assertive and believe you can do it and you are more than halfway there. Use the advice in this chapter to learn to draw the positives from pressure, and to manage it more effectively. You'll soon find that, far from crumbling under pressure, you will thrive on it.

# NINE

# HOW TO MAXIMISE YOUR TIME

## GOALS

- ☑ to maximise your use of time
- ☑ to spend more time on the things that matter
- ☑ to save time
- ☑ to avoid wasting time
- ☑ to delegate
- ☑ to learn how to say no

## HOW MUCH TIME HAVE YOU GOT?

If you feel like you're too busy to read this chapter, then you really need to read this chapter. Louis Armstrong once sang that 'we have all the time in the world'. If your time is taken up by bringing up children and holding down a full-time job while trying to maintain some semblance of a social life, you might like to take issue with Mr

161

Armstrong. But in truth, he's right. We all start life with the same amount of time – it's what we do with it that counts.

Of course, if we want to be a successful professional, partner and parent while perfecting our tennis game, learning French and helping out with the homeless at the local soup kitchen, then we might struggle. There might not be enough time to do everything we *want* to do, but winners know there is enough time to do everything we *need* to do.

'Live each day as if it were your last' might be an inspiring fridge magnet but, taken literally, it's not the most practical advice. You probably wouldn't ever go to work for starters. But the idea of making the most of your time is never a waste of time.

If you feel busy, that's a good sign. Having things to do is what keeps life exciting and rewarding. As we discovered in Chapter 8, busy people are usually more productive than non-busy people. They tend to work at their peak and prioritise effectively.

## YOU'VE ALWAYS GOT MORE TIME THAN YOU FEEL YOU HAVE

How busy do you feel right now? When it comes to our perception of time, how we feel is a huge factor. We can get very stressed and complain that there simply aren't enough hours in the day and we'll never get everything done – and risk burning out. Or we can change gear and get quite excited about the challenges ahead, and use the time pressure to govern the speed of our performance. Of course, to continue the analogy until it runs out of gas, some people floor it and end up speeding everywhere, eventually having a nasty accident – a stress-induced heart attack, or a realisation that they have missed their kids growing up. Others amble about at a dreamily slow pace, getting nowhere fast while life passes them by.

Just as an engine has an optimum speed, so do we. This chapter is going to teach you how to stay within the speed limit and maintain the best possible level of performance while enjoying the ride.

Winners know that those who get stressed about how much they've got to do often waste time and energy in the process. If you feel like you're going to miss a deadline, the worst thing you can do is panic. Just get on with what you can in the time available and you'll surprise yourself with how much you do. Those who resolve to tackle their list of tasks with relish usually maximise the time available. Winners know: you can only do your best – just make sure you do.

How we feel is a choice. Just as we can choose to be an optimist rather than a pessimist (see Chapter 2) and we can choose to stay calm rather than get stressed (see Chapter 8), so we can choose to make the best use of our time. By choosing to think differently, we can completely change how we feel. For that reason, winners have a different perception of time when getting very stressed: under pressure there is always more time than you feel there is. Just knowing that is calming in itself.

## TO DO: What kind of time manager are you?

Carefully consider the following statements, circling A or B, whichever is most true for you.

### 1. Meetings and appointments
A. I am usually early or on time.
B. I am usually late or almost late.

### 2. Deadlines
A. I usually complete them by the deadline without too much panic.
B. I tend to be very pushed for time, sometimes not finishing tasks before the deadline.

**3. Workload**

A. I have a manageable amount to do.

B. I always seem to have too much to do.

**4. Reputation**

A. People know that I am reliable and trustworthy when it comes to time.

B. I have a reputation for bad time management.

**5. Ability to say no**

A. I have no problem turning things down if I am too busy.

B. I tend to say yes, even if I am already swamped.

**6. Ability to plan**

A. I try and plan my time properly so that I can stick to deadlines.

B. I just get on with it and see how it pans out.

**7. Ability to delegate**

A. I divide up the workload where possible to increase efficiency.

B. I tend to do it all myself if I want it done properly.

**8. Ability to get started**

A. Once I've got a plan, I get cracking.

B. I find it frustratingly hard to get started and often find myself distracted.

**9. Ability to finish**

A. I always complete my tasks on time and then move on to the next thing.

B. I've always got a few things on the go that are half-done.

**10. Ability to multi-task**

A. I can cope with several things going on at once if necessary.

B. I can only really concentrate on one thing at a time.

### The results

**Mostly As**

Your time management doesn't seem to be too bad but it could still be improved: time is one of those things you can never have enough of. Have a look at any areas where you scored yourself a B and resolve to concentrate on improving those areas first as you work through this chapter. As you probably know, prioritising is one of the main strengths of an effective time manager.

**Mostly Bs**

Your time management could be improved but don't worry: you've come to the right place. This chapter is full of tips and techniques to help you make better use of your time. Plenty of them require quite simple adjustments. Invest some time and effort working on your bad habits in the short term and you'll save yourself much more time and effort in the long run.

# NO TIME TO THINK

When we're rushed and under pressure, we often panic and either freeze or make a snap decision. This is when we act on autopilot, on intuition only, and just do instinctively whatever feels right at the time without thinking about it. Consider how often you have made a silly mistake when you have rushed too much. The chances of success in such situations are small.

Since winners work to maximise their chances of success, they understand that the winning behaviours of T-CUP – Thinking

Correctly Under Pressure – are the most important and effective techniques at their disposal. It is precisely when under pressure that we need to think. Admittedly, it's hard to do it at first, but this is where the winning behaviours of T-CUP and the winning model (warrior–thinker–skill refiner–continuous debriefer) fit together. So when under pressure, hold on. Start by reminding yourself of the winning mantra: 'Under pressure I have more time than I feel I have.' Now you can think. Keep trying until it becomes second nature, until your instinct is to think before you act.

*When you feel like you're acting without taking time to think first, do a double-take. Ask yourself if this is an informed decision or a snap decision; a lasting, effective solution or a quick-fix.*

People sometimes report failure when they think too much or have too much time to think – like the striker who thinks too much about where to place a penalty and then gets caught in two minds; the house buyer who waits too long before making an offer and ends up losing out; the lover who overanalyses and invents problems in a relationship that aren't there by allowing destructive thoughts to run haywire. But in each case, the thinker has taken their mind off the immediate focus (scoring, buying, staying together) and is thinking about the possible negative consequences (missing, losing out, splitting up). You can avoid this by keeping the following in mind:

▶ Maintain focus on what you can control.
▶ Don't dwell on the negatives, the maybes, the things that might never happen.
▶ Maintain one-step-ahead thinking and visualise success in these situations and your chances of winning are greatly increased.

Why? Because when you feel capable, you are mentally prepared to mobilise your systems to bring about success.

---

## THINK: No time-wasters please

You might feel you never have enough time. Raise awareness of your time-wasting behaviour and you might be able to claw some spare time back. You will probably discover a pattern of wastefulness that can be improved. Are you always losing your keys? Put up a key hook. Are you always forgetting your toothbrush when you go away? Make a checklist of things to pack. Are you always 20 minutes late? So leave 20 minutes earlier. This is all part of the winning method of editing out your faults to reduce your frequency of failure and increase your frequency of success. You need to design yourself an efficient system that means that you don't waste time.

1. Think of three ways you wasted time yesterday. Perhaps you spent too long checking email. Maybe you missed a train and had to wait for the next one.

2. Now think of three more ways in which you often waste time. Do you watch too much rubbish on television? Are you always forgetting things when you leave the house and have to come back for them? Or do you tend to feel like you have more time than you really do, often making you late for appointments? List your common personal time-wasters on your 'problem pages' in Chapter 1. We're going to deal with them.

---

# HAVE YOU GOT A SECOND?

There are of course times when you have only a split second to react. Perhaps when someone in the car ahead brakes or swerves suddenly; someone puts you on the spot by asking you a difficult question; you think you've got 'house' at bingo. Then you might have to act on instinct – but as we learned in Chapter 7, you can train your instinct so that when you're put on the spot, you can make the right decision in the time available.

People sometimes achieve success when they appear to act on instinct or without really trying: 'I didn't think about it – I just did it.' When this happens it is because they are not allowing their mind to run away with them. As soon as you think about the consequences of your actions, the pressure mounts: 'What if I miss…?' 'What if she says "no"…?' 'Would that way be better…?' Self-doubt can usefully stop us doing reckless things and taking unnecessary risks, but it can also be very limiting. If we never venture out of our comfort zone, we'll never stretch ourselves. When people report success 'without even thinking about it', it's the possibility of failure that they are not thinking about. They are demonstrating 'one-step-ahead thinking' only, concentrating on their target and what they can control: 'I'll just do this and not consider all the possible ramifications that I cannot control.' As a result, they are not putting themselves under unnecessary pressure.

You can train yourself to do this. Jonny Wilkinson had only a split second to make that World Cup-winning drop goal, but he had made the decision to do it long before and had trained to do it that quickly for years. So he actually managed to squeeze a lot of time into that split second, and guess what: it paid off. If someone jams their brakes on, you know how to perform a safe emergency stop because you've practised it. You can prepare answers for a difficult question or develop stock ways of answering that stall for time or fire the question back, just as politicians do.

## TOO MUCH TIME?

Sometimes it's possible to have too much time on our hands – and this also requires winning time management.

Time often concertinas to fit the deadline. This is why a task that can take an hour when you're busy suddenly takes all day when you've got nothing else to do. Clearly this is an inefficient use of time, and it also might not elicit the best results because you won't have been performing at a peak level.

The trick here is to invent a deadline for yourself. Don't leave everything till the last minute and stress yourself out. Instead, plan something fun to do after you have finished your task. Then instead of spending all day spring cleaning the house, you can get it all done in the morning and enjoy the afternoon seeing that exhibition you promised yourself you'd go to. Instead of taking hours to process that paperwork while actually surfing the net and making endless cups of tea, give yourself an hour to blitz it and then you can spend the next hour at the gym. The sense of accomplishment and time well-spent is extremely rewarding.

Sometimes when the deadline is far off, there is no sense of urgency, no need to rush. Without adequate motivation from the adrenaline kick of time pressure, we can ignore the task for too long. This is especially problematic if the task is a big one: completing a thesis, renovating a house or planning a huge event. If we don't start early enough, suddenly we will be swamped with too much to do and not enough time to do it. And that leads to overwhelming stress. The task begins to control you rather than the other way round.

The trick here is to split the millstone into milestones. Break up the task into manageable chunks and give each a deadline. Perhaps write the deadlines down in your diary or stick them on the fridge. Be strict with yourself – deadlines should not be made out of elastic. Giving yourself an external deadline can also help (see page 173). Encouraged by a sense of progression rather than feeling weighed down by a sense of guilt and foreboding, you'll accomplish your task in time without stress and you will feel fantastic for doing so.

# THE IMPORTANCE OF PRIORITIES

*Do you really need to reply to that email now? Should you answer that phone call? Do you have to write up the minutes of that meeting, or could you delegate it?*

Doing what we need to do and what we'd like to do are often two very different things.

Some days, time seems to just evaporate and we haven't done all the things we needed to. Several items on our to-do list remain unticked, to be added to tomorrow's. We feel like we're chasing our tail but never get any closer to it. On other days, we steam through tasks as if we're a machine.

Why?

Distractions are usually to blame. Things are always going to crop up, especially if we work in a busy office or live in a hectic house. The phone will ring, people will ask us questions, we'll be called into meetings...

The number one rule in time management is prioritisation. This means arranging and organising your day in advance. You will need to draw up a timetable listing tasks in order of importance with realistic deadlines for each one. The number two rule in time management is sticking to this timetable come what may.

It's amazing how often and how easily we can be distracted by matters that are usually not all that urgent. For instance:

▶ Most emails can wait to be dealt with all in one go during a timetabled half-hour slot.
▶ Most phone calls or text messages can be returned when it suits you.
▶ Most meetings can be timetabled in advance.
▶ Most television programmes can be recorded to watch later.

Don't be afraid to shut yourself off from the distractions of the outside world occasionally. If we plan our time effectively and keep ourselves free from interruption, it's amazing how much we can accomplish in a short space of time. It's also important to maintain concentration and not allow ourselves to get bored or the task to run on and on without a deadline.

Winners know that in order to succeed they must 'avoid unnecessary corners' such as poor time management. This means that they will not allow themselves to be easily distracted from their tasks and will delegate where necessary. This requires the self-discipline of a warrior, but before long it will become a natural good habit. Decide on the essential basics that only you can deal with and then prioritise. You have to be tough: only emergencies can supersede the schedule. Constant winning debriefing will tell you whether or not you need to reassess your priorities.

One of my clients is the editor-in-chief of a very successful magazine. His editing style is to be very hands-on, and to be available at all times to his staff so that the production of the magazine is never held up – a method he learned from his old editor. However, the constant interruptions made it difficult for him to concentrate and maintain his train of thought. We fixed the problem with the simplest of solutions: the door to his office. When it was open, his staff could talk to him. When it was closed, he was not to be disturbed unless the matter was extremely important. As a result, his time management has become much more efficient and productive. So simple, yet so effective.

## MAKING PLANS

Here's how to get yourself organised:

## PLAN IN BLOCKS OF 30 MINUTES

Don't give yourself half-day chunks to complete tasks. You'll soon start to dawdle and daydream. Instead, chop and change regularly. If 30 minutes is not appropriate, you can work in hour-long blocks (for example, 55 minutes' work, 5-minute break), but this should be the maximum time span. Research suggests that the concentration span of the average adult is between 30 and 40 minutes. Time-blocking prevents boredom, keeps the pace and efficiency of work high and enables you to multitask.

## PLAN TO BE REALISTIC

You're not going to write a novel, cook a dinner party *and* complete 15 appraisal forms in one day. Break up the tasks you have to do into manageable and quantifiable goals that can be achieved in 30 minutes. Being able to tick off lots of small tasks is far more satisfying and motivating than ticking off one or none. Also, be specific. Writing general things like 'Do paperwork' is not measurable or quantifiable, whereas 'Input January invoices into spreadsheet and send to finance dept' is better.

## PLAN TO MOVE ON

Spending an age on one small detail is not an efficient way to work when time is precious. Consider the Pareto principle, an economist's theory which states that 80 per cent of the results come from 20 per cent of the effort. Get the 80 per cent done before you start perfecting the task with the remaining 20 per cent. Write the report before you start worrying about how to add pretty tables and graphs. If the bedroom is a mess, make the bed and open the windows first before you start dusting the skirting board.

## PLAN FOR A CHANGE OF PLAN

As with every plan, it would be wise to build in a degree of flexibility in case tasks over-run, or in case the boss suddenly calls you into their office. Rather than throw the whole schedule out of kilter, factor in some realistic slack time to cater for such eventualities and you will stay on track more easily.

## PLAN TO BE SPONTANEOUS

Preplanning as much as possible gives you more scope for being spontaneous. Being well on top of your workload means you'll be able to find time to take on an unplanned task or special project. Without preplanning, you might be forced to turn it down, or you might accept it and get yourself in trouble later.

## PLAN TO GET STARTED

Getting started is often the hardest bit. Don't spend forever drawing up the plan. This is a classic form of procrastination, beloved of revision students with colouring pencils. A jotted list on a piece of paper will do. You can buy 'To Do List' pads from most stationers. Give yourself five minutes to draw up the plan and then get started.

## PLAN TO AN EXTERNAL DEADLINE

Don't just rely on your own self-discipline to see you through. Tell other people what you are intending to do to encourage you to stick to your timetable rather than slacken off. Whether you're starting a new business, training for a marathon, trying to lose weight or simply motoring through your workload, the social pressure that comes from the expectations and the 'How are you getting on?' questions of others is very motivating.

## PLAN A REWARD

Once you have achieved your list of goals, give yourself a reward. It's important that you enjoy your successes, that you live in the now. It might be as simple as a short tea break once that paperwork is out of the way, or it might be a celebratory dinner with your partner once a big project is completed. Make the size of the reward – and the length of any time off – commensurate with the size of the task completed. And only allow yourself to have the reward on completion of the work. Don't say, 'I'll sunbathe for half an hour and then start.' The reward will feel much better if you know you've earned it.

## PLAN FOR THE FUTURE

As part of your continuous debrief, have you learned anything that could make life easier in future? Does working with a tidy desk make you more efficient? Does switching the phone to divert and turning off your email help you concentrate? Does filing your bills make it easier to keep track of them? Does taking time to explain yourself properly from the start mean you have fewer time-sapping questions to answer later? Build in the lessons you have learned for next time by adding them to your 'basics' of winning time management.

## TO DO: I love it when a plan comes together

Using as many of the above tips as possible, get a sheet of paper and draw up a plan for tomorrow. Feel the satisfaction of ticking tasks off and make sure you reward yourself appropriately. Debrief and evaluate how you did at the end of the day. Were you able to complete your list? If not, why not? Were the tasks too unrealistic? How can you learn from this for next time? Incorporate the improvements in another plan for the following day and so on, until planning and adhering to those plans becomes a habit.

# THE ART OF DELEGATION

Winners are good at delegating because they appreciate the value of effective teamwork. We probably all spend hours doing things that others perhaps could and should do. This is especially true the higher up in life we go and the more responsibility we take on. So as we begin to reap the rewards of living a winning way of life, delegation will become increasingly important.

Some of us are reluctant to hand over tasks to others. Perhaps we are perfectionists or we are over-controlling. Or maybe we subscribe too strongly to the maxim that 'if you want something done properly, do it yourself'. If you are of this mindset, fight against it like the warrior you are.

The managing director of a chain of coffee shops taught me something about delegation. He built a great team of committed people around him whom he could entrust to look after different aspects of managing the company – responsibilities that most MDs would see as part of their personal job description. This allowed him to oversee the whole operation more easily, and enabled him to devote more time and energy to the areas in which he was especially skilled or which needed particular attention. It gave him flexibility and the ability to see the bigger picture. If he hadn't delegated, he wouldn't have been able to achieve all that was required of him. By empowering and entrusting his staff through effective delegation, he found that they responded by conscientiously embracing their responsibilities. The result was an efficient, productive, proud and happy workforce.

Delegating immediately frees up time for you to spend on more crucial tasks, or on being creative in your field of expertise – or perhaps it'll just help you get out of the office that bit earlier of an evening. It therefore improves your quality of life and of work. It also allows you the time to think, to listen, to absorb, to develop and to enjoy what it is you are doing.

Effective, winning delegation is not a lazy option where you take advantage of others. Winners do not operate in isolation, and they don't jeopardise team harmony and the ethic of togetherness. Winners draw positively on the strengths and competence of others in striving for success.

---

**THINK: Who could do that?**

Whether it's at work, at your sports club or at home, draw up your list of responsibilities and discuss with others whether there is anything from the list that they could take on. This isn't merely a case of dumping work on others; often people are only too pleased to be given a sense of responsibility and control as long as their own workload doesn't become unreasonable.

If there is no one to whom you can delegate, find people to ease the burden, even if it's only in the capacity of a sounding board. Train up people to take on tasks: this is an effective use of time in the long run.

---

## LEARN TO SAY 'NOT NOW'

If you want to reassert control over your time and commitments and therefore your life, you need to be able to say 'not now' – people will respect you a lot more than if you were just a ' yes-man'. But it can be very difficult to say for a number of reasons:

▶ We don't like to appear to let people down, especially if it might have consequences.
▶ We don't like to appear as if we can't manage to do everything.
▶ We don't like arguments so we'll say 'yes' to keep the peace.
▶ We don't have the confidence to stand up for ourselves.
▶ We don't want to disappoint ourselves.

▶ We don't want the work to go to a colleague who would then get the credit for it.

▶ We don't want to pass up the opportunity to learn something new or interesting.

The problem is that being a 'yes-man' can be an even worse reputation to have. Remember that 'nice guys often finish last'. It means people take advantage of your good nature, or think of you as a soft touch. People often say 'yes' when they can't think of how to say 'no' so this is yet another example where T-CUP comes in handy.

Being able to say 'not now' demonstrates a level of assertiveness, self-respect and self-confidence that every winner needs and others will respect. It means you're not afraid to stand up for yourself, to push back, to force the other party to find a better solution than dumping everything at your doorstep. It helps you feel more in control of your life, and less like someone else's puppet. This gives us what psychologists call an 'internal locus of control'.

Saying 'not now' also means that you don't overstretch yourself to the point where you get very stressed or the quality of your work dips – alongside your enjoyment. It helps you to maintain your standards and sense of control over what you do. And saying 'not now' helps us manage our time much more easily. So when something important to you comes up – such as a family commitment or a friend who needs your help – you are more likely to be able to say 'yes'.

There are ways of saying 'not now', of course. Saying a straight 'no' without giving a reason isn't likely to go down very well. But nor is coming up with an implausible sob story or list of excuses. A firm but diplomatic and reasoned 'not now' is likely to be most effective: it's not easy to talk round and it sounds considered rather than selfish. You could also try suggesting an alternative solution. You can adapt the following example for your own purposes:

*I'm sorry, normally I would help, but I can't on this occasion because I've already made plans that I simply mustn't break. But I appreciate this is important, so would you like me to ask around to see if anyone else can step in?*

---

## THINK: Should I have done that?

Think of something you agreed to do recently that you'd really rather not have done because you were short on time. (Visiting your aunt in hospital is not a good example. Staying late after work for the third Friday in a row when you had a dinner party to go to is a better one.) Ask yourself the following debriefing questions:

1. What did I want to happen? *To say 'not now' because I was supposed to be doing something else.*
2. What actually happened? *I was caught at a bad moment and said 'yes' instead of 'not now'.*
3. What made you do this? *I'm afraid of losing people's sympathy by refusing them.*
4. What are you going to do about it next time? *I'll bear in mind that by saying 'no' the right way I'll buy sympathy and respect from others. I'll say 'not now'.*

---

# ADD ANOTHER 10 MINUTES

Plan for things not going to plan. People with poor time management often misjudge or underestimate the amount of time something is going to take. This is one instance where a pessimistic viewpoint can help. Traffic lights will not always be on green when you're in a rush; the dodgy printer won't always produce the report 30 seconds before the meeting; and your boss has a nasty habit of saying, 'Before you go, would you mind doing this last thing?'

Thinking this way is down to bad habits and lack of thought, debriefing and learning from past mistakes. You might have got away with winging it in the past, so you think you can do so again. In such instances you need to buy yourself more time.

If it takes 10 minutes to get to the train station on a good day, then don't assume you can get it down to eight if you run. Give yourself 20 minutes. Then you won't leave your ticket at home in the panic.

If you are running unavoidably late – and it happens to us all from time to time – then phone ahead and add 10 minutes on top of your new estimated time of arrival in case of further delays. This takes the pressure off for both parties because you are no longer panicking and they are no longer expecting.

Adding this buffer doesn't give you *carte blanche* to eat into the extra time unnecessarily, however. The extra 10 minutes is like an emergency credit card – you use it only when you really have to.

---

## Quick fix

Don't have time to read the whole chapter? Then just take these time-saving tips for now:

### Work backwards

When planning how much time something is going to take you and how you are going to achieve your goal, work backwards from the deadline. Make sure you factor in an extra 10 minutes to account for any possible problems or delays.

### Work quickly

Economists say you can do 80 per cent of the task with 20 per cent of

---

the effort. Get the majority of the task done before you start perfecting it. A winner always gets the best possible result in the time available.

**Work to completion**

A job half-done is a full waste of time. So adapt the *Mastermind* rule of thumb: 'I've started so I'll finish... properly.' This is the essence of stage two of the winning behaviour cycle: seizing the opportunity the winning way.

## TO DO: A winning time

### 1. Work towards straight As

Return to the questionnaire at the start of this chapter and consider how what you have read can help you address your problem areas. Resolve to make every effort to improve by setting yourself quantifiable, measurable targets. If you are always late for work, for example, promise yourself that you will count how many times you are early and how many times you are late per week. Make a note in your diary for a month's time to come back and do the questionnaire again to see how your results have improved. Keep debriefing and working at it like a winner.

### 2. Count on yourself

Return to your list of common time-wasters and draw up a plan for dealing with them. If you always forget something when you leave the house, lay everything out the night before – phone, keys, money, gym kit, book. If you spend too much time watching television, playing computer games or sitting in the pub, make an effort to spend less time doing that; instead, use the time you save to do something more worthwhile, like phoning your parents, going for a run or reading a Booker prize-winner. You'll feel better about yourself and your use of time.

# HAVE THE TIME OF YOUR LIFE

As you will, I hope, now understand, there are no great miracles when it comes to managing your time effectively. It's just about making simple and pragmatic changes – exactly as winners do in each part of life. Improving time management is about raising our awareness of what regularly wastes our time and what generates time. It's also about changing our habits and our thinking – and that takes time. Understanding the logic is the easy part. Putting it into practice is where the warrior spirit comes in. Life isn't too short if you don't waste it. Use the tips in this chapter but, as with everything in this book, don't expect it to become second nature overnight – that's half the point. Take your time.

# TEN

# GO FORTH AND WIN

## GOALS

- ☑ to see the application of the winning model in our own lives
- ☑ to draw up a personal, workable, winning life plan of action
- ☑ to start winning – now!

## TAKE WINNING TO ANOTHER DIMENSION

Chapters 1 to 9 laid out clearly all the pieces of the jigsaw puzzle – now we need to fit them together to see the bigger picture: a winning way of life. Using these individual skills in isolation will work to an extent, but combining them all will take us to another dimension of winning – one where we experience success frequently rather than occasionally.

Getting used to a new way of doing things may feel slightly odd at first and require a bit of thought, especially if you have to overwrite old bad habits. That's what makes a warrior. It's a bit like learning a new, more effective backhand technique in tennis when you're used to your old ways. The new method will take a bit of getting used to and a little practice but you'll start seeing the benefits as soon as you apply the new principles. Before long, as the memory muscle kicks in, you'll stop thinking about it and it will feel perfectly natural. So it is with winning. There comes a stage where you reach your personal tipping point, after which everything feels natural and gathers its own momentum. The winning behaviours become contagious; they spread to other parts of your life. Give these techniques a chance and, when you see how they work, they'll soon become second nature.

Then, eventually, there is even a third dimension. What this book gives you is a winning model. The whole point of it is that you can follow the model and develop it for your own purposes. It's like learning anything – how to play that backhand, drive a car, speak Swahili... Once you have mastered the basic rules and techniques, you can then develop them to continue your improvement. It will take a bit of time and practice to get to this stage, just as it would to become a great driver, accomplished musician or fluent linguist. But follow the warrior – thinker – skill refiner – continuous debriefer model into which the winning behaviours of T-CUP fit and you will be able to adapt my method to create your own bespoke version. So long as you adhere to the winning principles when you develop, you can't really go wrong.

For now, though, let's concentrate on fitting all the pieces together into a coherent and practical life plan.

## THINKING LIKE A WINNER

The bedrock of winning is a belief that we can change the way we think and behave if we put our minds to it. And this includes the belief that we deserve to be winners.

Many people tend to think that their personality is set in stone from birth, but the fact is that we choose to change the way we think and behave all the time. We're heavily influenced by our environment, by the people in our lives, by what we are exposed to – and yes, by what we read. It's all part of human interaction and development. Just think of the last expensive restaurant you ate at, or film you went to see. In how many cases was your thinking and behaviour influenced by another's recommendation?

I'm not trying to turn people into winning clones. If anything, I believe the winning model increases your number of options and gives you greater potential to be autonomous rather than an automaton. Winners believe that life is what they make of it, not what life makes of them. They believe that talent can be developed and abilities improved over time, and that opens up many more possibilities. People who think this way:

- ▶ tend to feel more in control of their lives and their destinies
- ▶ are not dictated to by circumstance or by other people
- ▶ are active rather than passive
- ▶ capitalise on their opportunities: 'they make a lot of what they've got'.

The strength of their 'I will' power and their positive vocabulary means that they focus on what they can do and control. This leads to improvement: increased frequency of success and decreased frequency of failure. The approach is more optimistic: failure is chalked up to experience, something to be learned from, because 'winning doesn't happen in a straight line'. Success based deliberately on the winning principles is seen as confirmation that everything is on the right track rather than as a stroke of luck.

And yet the changes required are not huge. They're not going to radically alter who you are as a person; they're just going to change how much success you have and how much you enjoy life as a whole. Small changes, big results.

---

## The aim of the game

Just as you are returning to the goals you set yourself when you began reading this book, so let's look back at what this book set out to do. The aim was to persuade you to see the truth of this statement (see page 3):

*You don't need to be naturally talented to be a winner. You don't need to be hyper-intelligent to do well. You don't need to be highly skilled to be successful. You don't need to be rich to have an advantage in life. Of course all of these things can help, but whoever you are and whatever it is you want to achieve, you can quite easily be one of life's winners – irrespective of natural talent, intelligence and great skill.*

To that end, the aims of this book have been to give you:
1. the assurance that you are **capable and deserving** of being one of life's winners, irrespective of talent, intellect or skill
2. the **confidence and self-belief** to enable you to think like a winner
3. a clear insight into the **logic behind success** and the reason for failure
4. the **awareness** of what you do when you succeed and what you do when you fail
5. tips to help you succeed more often and take **proactive control** of your life
6. tools to help you refine your winning behaviours (skills) and further develop my principles for your own purposes in order to truly **maximise your potential**

---

7. the optimistic **enthusiasm** and creative, proactive **drive** to put the theory into practice, to make it happen the winning way.

Ultimately, the aim is to make you happier and more satisfied with your life through achieving more success and experiencing less failure.

# BE A GOAL-GETTER

At the start of the book, you were asked to think about your desired goals – what you want to achieve in life. Successful people are focused people who know what they want and what they are working towards. Make sure you have a measurable goal in life and take control of it – don't just drift along and see what happens. Aim for 100 per cent and you may score 90 per cent or more. Settle for 70 per cent and you may come out with a very average score.

In Chapter 3 you gave yourself a percentage mark for the areas of your life that mean the most to you, or which you feel you need to address. Now is a good time to refer back to those marks (see page 56) to see if they have improved or not. The goal is to keep working at them, and to keep improving.

Winning is also about looking to the future: 'Where do you see yourself in 5, 10 or 15 years' time?' This is a classic interview question for a good reason. It immediately shows whether or not you are a goal-getter. Do you want to have moved on to bigger and better things, or are you happy to stay precisely where you are now? Do you want to have a successful career, a happy and healthy home life, money in the bank, great holidays, the respect of others, good friends? Then make it happen – now.

Good habits are hard to make. Many of us are good at making New Year's resolutions but few of us are so good at keeping them. It needn't be that way. Research has proven that failure to keep to our good intentions is most often due to the following factors:

▶ the targets were not thought through properly
▶ the targets were not measurable enough
▶ the commitment was not strong enough.

## MAKE TIME TO THINK

Don't leave life to fate. Spend some proper time drawing up your life plan using the tips below. Don't just dash off a quick plan in a frenzied half-hour of inspiration. Perhaps use the head space of a week's holiday to really consider what you want to focus on and how you want to do it. Follow the winning behaviour cycle. Go through each area of your life and spend some time thinking about it. Instead of coming back from a week's holiday just with a tan that will fade, you could return with a plan that will last and a new lease of life, refreshed, refocused and ready to take on the world.

## MAKE IT QUANTIFIABLE

When drawing up your goals, make them defined and measurable targets rather than generic notions. Follow the idea of 'creating the opportunity for your desired success'. Make a list of the preconditions necessary for achieving your desired goals. Then, by continuously debriefing, you can monitor how well you're doing, set target deadlines, schedule appointments in your diary and generally make it a lot easier to see a sense of progression and avoid periods of plateau. If you don't know whether you're making headway, you won't stick with it. Make your goals realistic and then make them real.

| GENERIC NOTION – woolly ideas | DEFINED TARGET – 'I will' power |
|---|---|
| Save money. | I will set up a standing order of £50 each week into a subsidiary account I cannot easily access: £50 x 52 weeks = £2,600. |
| Get a promotion. | I will ask the boss for an appraisal to define new job targets, and schedule a performance and pay review in three months' time. |
| Be a better parent. | I will devote Saturday mornings to the kids, and schedule activities such as visits to the park, the swimming pool and the shops. |
| Lose weight. | I will lose two pounds per week for three months: 2 x 12 weeks = 24 pounds = over 1½ stone. |
| Improve timekeeping. | I will never be late for work again and I will arrange early-morning meetings to help me achieve this. |
| Cut down on smoking. | I will commit to giving up totally on this specific date and ask all my friends and family for help and support. The money I save over a year from not smoking (say, £1,800) I will put towards a new car. |

## MAKE A COMMITMENT

Finding the self-discipline to stick to your goals can be tough. Make it easier in the long term by being tougher in the short term. Force yourself to write down your goals in a clear manner. Research claims that it takes five weeks for lasting habits to form. You don't necessarily have to make year-long commitments. Just go for five weeks initially, and then see how you're doing.

## MAKE REVISIONS

Looking back on your achievements is a satisfying and healthy form of debriefing. You certainly don't need to write a diary as such, but perhaps you could keep your lists of goals to look back on and see what you have achieved and how your priorities have changed. Look at it as an ever-developing personal CV of winning. Each year you need to be able to look back and see achievements that you are proud of, not regrets and 'if onlys'. Seeing such obvious changes by looking at the contrasting 'before and after' pictures will give you a sense of satisfaction and the motivation to carry on. Knowing where you have come from will help you determine where you are going.

## MAKE A START

Whatever you do, make sure you start doing it. There are too many planners in life and not enough doers. So once you have prepared properly, get on with it. You can only do your best – just make sure you do.

## MAKE IT LAST

Maintain the momentum. Don't rest on your laurels or allow complacency to set in, nor should you ever admit defeat. Two great quotes from Winston Churchill spring to mind here. The first is:

'Never, never, never give up.' The second is: 'Success is not final, failure is not fatal: it is the courage to continue that counts.'

# FROM PROBLEM PAGES
# TO SUCCESS STORY

On the 'problem pages' at the beginning of the book (or in a separate notebook) you jotted down your goals and areas you wanted to work on so that you could focus on them while reading, and add to them as you progressed through the book. (If you haven't done this yet, do it now. Go to page 22 to see how.) Now we're going to work on how to tackle those areas of focus so that you can see a 'before and after' effect of using the tools and techniques in this book. The idea is to leave you with a practical and usable life plan-of-action.

The following are examples of how you might create the opportunity for your desired success, setting out the required preconditions. These are not necessarily templates, merely idea germinators to help you. Have a look at them, then draw up your own that make use of the winning way to help you achieve your desired goals.

Remember: writing down your thoughts helps to give them focus and purpose. It also enables you to see a sense of progression and development. Reading is passive; thinking and writing are active.

## EXAMPLE 1

**Area:** CAREER

**Desired success:** To get a promotion

**Other desired goals:** A sizeable pay rise; an increase in responsibility; a five-year career progression plan

**Creating the opportunity:**

▶ Relationship with boss: gain trust, confidence and take interaction beyond the superficial, go through job description/my basics

▶ Assertiveness and involvement: discuss plans with boss and show him that I have ambition, initiative and leadership potential, ask for an appraisal/feedback (formal debrief)

▶ Deadlines: show him that I can get good quality work done on time, set a deadline of six months

▶ Timekeeping: work at ensuring I am at my desk by 9am each day

▶ Communication with colleagues: take a more proactive, participatory role in the team; demonstrate positive enthusiasm

**Seizing the opportunity:**

▶ Think positively

▶ Apply my game plan:

i. Develop my relationship with my boss – get more in his eye line for positive reasons

ii. Show quantifiable improvement and dedication worthy of promotion over a target period of three months with a view to getting the recognition within the following three months

iii.  Identify the corners

iv.  Look at my job description and ensure that I am satisfying it at a base level

▶ Stick to what works and thus maximise any areas in which I am excelling:

i.  Keep up my proven time management techniques

ii.  Stick to my proven communication style with my colleagues

▶ Continue to debrief and target any areas in which I am falling short:

i.  Be more positive and proactive – rather than a passive passenger

ii.  Increase my confidence and participation in meetings

iii.  Improve my performance in one-to-one situations with my boss; improve my performance in presentations

**Maintaining the momentum:**

▶ Generally show an attitude of enthusiasm, commitment and competence – adopt a winning mindset

▶ Get up earlier and get organised before bed

▶ Generate and pitch new ideas

▶ Schedule another meeting with my boss for three months' time to monitor progress and maintain momentum

## EXAMPLE 2

**Area:** FAMILY (also WORK/LIFE BALANCE)

**Desired success:** To develop a closer relationship with my sons

**Other desired goals:** To leave work on time; to leave work at work and not bring it home; to organise a family holiday

**Creating the opportunity:**
- ▶ Find time and increase availability
- ▶ Manage anger levels
- ▶ Take a more obvious interest in the kids' lives
- ▶ Boost energy levels
- ▶ Share responsibilities more fairly with partner
- ▶ Boost creativity
- ▶ Set a deadline: five weeks to form a habit, starting today
- ▶ Improve time management, efficiency and delegation skills
- ▶ Don't bring work home
- ▶ Look in the paper for weekend activities to do

**Seizing the opportunity:**
- ▶ Think positively
- ▶ Apply my game plan:
  - i.   Scale back work commitments
  - ii.  Improve time efficiency at work
  - iii. Improve discipline and self-control
- ▶ Stick to what works and thus maximise any areas in which I am excelling:
  - i.   Go to bed early to alleviate tiredness

ii. Leave work at 6pm to make myself available in the evenings to read stories/help with homework/play games

iii. Leave computer at work

▶ Set aside time for family

▶ Continue to debrief and target any areas in which I am falling short:

i. Be less distracted – answer emails and phone calls only in timetabled slots

ii. Delegate at work – train up a junior to take on responsibility

iii. Learn how to say not now to unreasonable requests

**Maintaining the momentum:**

▶ Book a week's holiday

▶ Don't take any improvement for granted, so set aside Saturday mornings or Sunday afternoons for family time

▶ Make home a work-free zone

▶ Set deadlines – divide up projects from the start with planned timetables

▶ Plan to be spontaneous – use a diary to book appointments such as a family outing to the cinema; taking sons to the football match; a week's holiday to a kid-friendly place; a camping weekend

# CAREER, MONEY AND WORK/LIFE BALANCE

# TIME MANAGEMENT, PLANNING AND ORGANISATION

## LOVE, FAMILY AND FRIENDS

# HEALTH, IMAGE AND SELF-ESTEEM

# MAKE THE MOST OF FAILURE

This book will not make you exempt from failure. But it will massively cut down your rate of failure and also make you immune to its negative effects.

Pete and Saira go on a skiing holiday. Pete has been several times before and is a decent skier but a fairly unadventurous one. He's scared of falling over so stays within his comfort zone. Saira has not been as often, but is prepared to push herself to improve and learn. Pete hardly falls over all week, but he hardly improves as a skier either. Saira has at least one fall every day but has a whale of a time, and by the end of the holiday she has made a vast, measurable improvement.

If you push yourself, you will fall from time to time. That is a good 'success from setbacks' attitude. What isn't healthy is when failure stops you, when you see it as 'proof' of your perceived 'incompetence'. Either you're too scared to try in the first place, or a bad experience inhibits you in the future. Both approaches represent a relatively low pain threshold, and this is something that can be worked on. A healthy response to failure and to a fear of failure is to say: 'Right, how can I improve? How can I make it better? Because I am determined to do so.' Once you're thinking in that proactive frame of mind, you naturally mobilise everything you need to make it happen. It feels as if there is nothing you cannot do. Failure or the fear of failure is normal. However, both should be a motivational drive to challenge you, to spur you on, to fire you up, to prove anyone who has ever doubted you wrong – including you. Focus on what you can do and what you can control – not what you can't – and you'll be amazed by the results.

As only strong people can admit their shortcomings and overcome them, winners recognise failure, deal with it, learn from it and so make a success of it. Any meaningful success doesn't happen in a straight line. It's neither a plateau nor a straight sky-rocketing line – it's a learning curve. There will be the occasional setback, but so long as the overall pattern is onwards and upwards then you are on the winning way.

# The power of positive thinking

Part of getting your winning mindset right is expecting success and then visualising it. Visualise achieving your goal; visualise coping well with any nerves and pressure; visualise what it will feel like, how you will feel afterwards, what effect it will have.

Make sure you can answer 'yes' to the following checklist of winning characteristics:

Are you...
Committed?
Motivated?
Driven?
Disciplined?
Adaptable?
Open-minded?
Resourceful?
Passionate?
Enthusiastic?
Diligent?
Proactive?
Optimistic?
Generous?
Thoughtful?
A go-getter?
Focused?

Build yourself up to achieve. Repeat words of encouragement – especially some key phrases from T-CUP. It may help to have a few easy-to-remember catchphrases (such as those on page 7) to repeat to yourself as a mantra to aid T-CUP.

# THE FINAL CHAPTER IN THE SUCCESS STORY

You've got the new design for life; it's time to start building it. You have the tools in this book; now use them. You have it within you to be one of life's winners, so what are you waiting for?

The one thing that separates winners from all the rest is drive:

▶ to maximise their potential
▶ to overcome obstacles
▶ to perform at their very best
▶ to improve all the time
▶ to make life as fulfilling as possible
▶ to make it happen.

Be proactive. Take control. Enjoy winning.

Many of the techniques will work straight away, which will be encouraging. Other changes may take some time. But by following the winning model – warrior, thinker, skill refiner, continuous debriefer – together with the winning behaviours of T-CUP you will develop the discipline and the patience to achieve the desired goals you have set yourself.

Do not mistake wishful thinking for positive thinking. The mistake many people make is to study the biggest achievers, hear how supremely confident they are about their chances of winning and confuse cause and effect. Winners don't win just because they think they will. It's a combination of desire, belief and diligence. We win because we want to win, and we've done everything we can to prepare for it according to the winning model. We work, think and practise like winners. That is why we maximise our potential.

The realisation of your goals might not happen overnight, but I guarantee it will happen much more quickly than it would otherwise.

This is because the awareness you have built up through debriefing and the winning behaviour techniques you have learned here will help you streamline and refine the winning process. This means that your route to success is much more efficient, with a much reduced risk of failure. It's not trial and error; it's trial and refinement. I promise you this: if you keep on debriefing all the time and acting on the lessons you learn in accordance with the winning principles in this book, you are guaranteed to experience real progress. Increasingly, you will discover that winning is not a sporadic or temporary experience, but a continuous and ongoing lifestyle.

This model will help give your life a structure around which you can build layer upon layer of success. Now that you can see how all the pieces of the jigsaw fit together, it's something to which you can refer back to make sure you are on the right track. I hope you will do precisely that – when you're feeling in need of some practical tips, or perhaps want to look again with pride in the coming months and see how far you have come. Because winning is an evolutionary process of continual development, I believe that you will find something new or encouraging in this book each time you dip into it.

This is the end of the book but it is not the final chapter. That's for you to write. You now control where things go from here. You can be the author of your own success story and you can create a happy and successful ending for yourself.

Be assured that you are one of life's winners. You've got the plan; you've got the mindset and the tools to implement it. Now it's time to get on with making it happen. Here's to your success!

# INDEX